LAND ON BOTH FEET

LAND ON BOTH FEET

A Skateboarder's 11 Lessons That Transition to Life

BRETT SOREM

Library Tales Publishing

www.LibraryTalesPublishing.com

www.Facebook.com/LibraryTalesPublishing

Copyright © 2025 by Brett Sorem

All Rights Reserved

Published in New York, New York.

No part of this publication may be reproduced, stored in a retrieval system, or transmitted in any form or by any means, electronic, mechanical, photocopying, recording, scanning, or otherwise, except as permitted under Sections 107 or 108 of the 1976 United States Copyright Act, without the prior written permission of the Publisher. Requests to the Publisher for permission should be addressed to the Legal Department: Legal@LibraryTales.com

Trademarks: Library Tales Publishing, Library Tales, the Library Tales Publishing logo, and related trade dress are trademarks or registered trademarks of Library Tales Publishing and/or its affiliates in the United States and other countries, and may not be used without written permission. All other trademarks are the property of their respective owners.

For general information on our other products and services, please contact our Customer Care Department at 1-800-754-5016, or fax 917-463-0892. For technical support, please visit www.LibraryTalesPublishing.com

Library Tales Publishing also publishes its books in a variety of electronic formats. Every content that appears in print is available in electronic books.

∼

9 7 9 8 8 9 4 4 1 0 2 0 3

Printed in the United States of America

Contents

Prologue	1
1. Push With Your Back Foot, The Rest Comes Naturally	3
2. The Balance of Hell and Harmony	18
3. We're Not Made of Glass	30
4. When One Door Closes, Grind the Steps	45
5. Respecting the Law Doesn't Mean You Shouldn't Break It	57
6. We're All In This Together	65
7. Battles Are Uphill, and the Peaks Are Made of Marble	77
8. Skill Isn't Measured by What You Can Do, but How You Do What You Can	91
9. Find Your Lane and Shred	104
10. Focus, Forget, and Always Land On Both Feet	111
11. The Last Try Is a New Beginning	126
The Final Push	132

Prologue

It wasn't until I found myself closer to forty than thirty that I realized life had snuck up on me. One moment, I was skating the streets of San Diego without a care in the world. The next, I had a mortgage, two kids, and a career I actually earned. Somewhere in between, I blinked, twenty years disappeared, and suddenly, I was a full-blown adult. Never imagined that would happen.

I've made my share of choices—some bold, some questionable—but one stands out more than the rest: trading my baseball glove for a skateboard. At the time, it felt like rebellion. My dad, who never missed a single game, looked crushed when I told him I wasn't trying out for my high school team. He believed I was destined for a college scholarship. I believed I was destined for something else.

Looking back, I know he was angry—not at me, exactly, but at the future he thought I was throwing away. And maybe I was. But if I had a time machine, I'd make the same choice every time. That skateboard didn't just define my teenage years; it shaped the person I am today. It taught me to embrace failure, value independence, and carve my own path—even when it wasn't the easy one.

This book is about those moments—the choices we make and the lives they create. It's about the kid I was, the adult I became, and the lessons I picked up on the board along the way. It's not perfect. Neither am I. But if you're reading this, maybe you'll find something here that resonates.

"Skateboarding doesn't make you a skateboarder; not being able to stop skateboarding makes you a skateboarder." ~ *Tony Hawk*

1

Push With Your Back Foot,
The Rest Comes Naturally

There aren't many rules in skateboarding. It's just you and your board. You choose the next move—not the game, not a coach, and definitely not your teammates. Every decision is yours and yours alone, and the consequences are yours to live with.

by the early 1980s, skateboarding was in a transitional phase. The wildly popular spectacle of the 1970s had faded, almost disappearing entirely by the time I took my first steps. Freestyle skateboarding, with its intricate tricks, was losing ground. The rebellious Dogtown Z-Boys culture had fizzled out. Tony Hawk was still a wiry kid ripping vert ramps in Carlsbad. Rodney Mullen, often called the father of modern skateboarding, was quietly reinventing the sport on his family farm in Gainesville. Without these two pioneers (and a small circle of like-minded innovators), skateboarding might have been lost to the Santa Ana winds by the time I was old enough to ride. Rodney Mullen, in particular, changed everything. By experimenting with the possibilities of popping an ollie, he laid the foundation for street skateboarding. What started as an underground movement grew slowly, but by the mid-1980s, skaters began to take their tricks to the streets. They adapted pool boards to grind curbs, slide rails, and flip tricks on flat ground.

This era is immortalized in the 1986 cult film *Thrashin'*, starring a young Josh Brolin, which reintroduced skateboarding to pop culture. Around the same time, the modern street skateboard—complete with concave, a nose, and a tail—was born. Skateboarding as we know it today began to take shape.

Fast forward twelve years from Rodney's invention of the kickflip, and the first ESPN *X-Games* debuted in 1995. Street skateboarding exploded into pop culture and hasn't stopped growing since. Back then, you could only find skateboard gear in niche skate shops. Now, even Versace makes a thousand-dollar skate shoe. And in 2021, skateboarding became an official Olympic sport. The journey from obscure subculture to global phenomenon has unfolded within my lifetime.

To me, skateboarding is more art than sport. A handrail, a painted curb, a loading dock, or a sewer ditch—things most people pass by without a second glance—are my canvas. The stroke of your foot, the pop of the tail, and the grind of the trucks combine to create something both beautiful and raw. With imagination, you can do almost anything.

Well... almost anything. Just, for the love of all that is holy, don't push Mongo.

Mongo

Let's get this out of the way: mongo pushers are skateboarders who push with their front foot. If you've been paying attention, you've seen them—aimlessly darting down sidewalks, looking unsteady, like they're one pebble away from disaster. For the record, when I say "we" from here on out, I'm talking about skateboarders. Not just anyone who happens to own a board, but those who are immersed in the culture. Important distinction: buying a skateboard, strolling down the boardwalk, and rocking gear from Tilly's doesn't make you a skateboarder. Sorry, but no.

For us, skateboarding is more than a hobby; it's a way of life. It defines who we are and gives voice to our inner rebel. Enough with societal norms—grab a board, bomb a hill, and let the wind slap you in the face until your worries blow away. At our core, skaters are suspicious of conformity, yet somehow skateboarding has become part of the mainstream. And that's fine by us—we can handle the spotlight. Come one, come all. There's no maximum capacity on this train. The more people who jump on board, the better it gets. More skate parks get built, more skate companies thrive, and more strangers finally understand who we are, what we're doing, and why we love it.

If you're a kid just starting out on your skateboarding journey, let me say this: I envy you. When old people claim they'd never go back to being young, they're lying. Trust me. To start over, to relive the excitement and stupidity of those early years, would be a gift. Enjoy every second of it. Try not to piss off your parents *too* much, though. They've literally done everything for you, and, believe it or not, they might actually know a thing or two about what you're going through.

And to the parents debating whether or not to let your kid skate: don't be an uptight prick. Skaters today aren't all potheads and degenerates like we were back in the day (okay, maybe some still are, but not *all*). Rebelling in your teens is a fundamental part of growing up. Let your kid figure things out—falling down and getting back up is what skateboarding (and life) is all about.

That said, here's one piece of unsolicited but absolutely critical parenting advice: the single most important thing you can do (besides buying their first board, of course) is make sure they push with their back foot—not their front foot. Not Mongo. Seriously. "Who taught you to push that way, your mom?" Spare yourself and your kid the embarrassment. Start them off right.

Mid-'90s

In the mid-'90s, mocking Mongo pushers was practically a sport in itself. Among us, they typically represented the "poser"—a species of skateboard owner more interested in looking cool than learning the culture. These were the kids who would rather slap a few stickers on their brand-new boards than spend a Saturday in the parking lot learning how it feels to eat pavement.

Kids who skate today have it easy. Skateboarding has seeped into mainstream culture, influencing fashion, music, and even luxury brands. From baggy jeans and oversized tees to punk streetwear and bulky skate shoes, much of what's now trendy originated in skateboarding. But back in high school, being a skater came with its fair share of ridicule. I remember the looks and the comments about my slim, almost girlish frame swimming in baggy clothes. My jeans were at least four sizes too big, held up by a shoelace cinched around my hips. My oversized T-shirt drooped past my elbows, and my Padres hat barely kept the tips of my hair in check. My shoes—ragged, oversized, and held together by sheer willpower—looked like they'd been through a war. But that was the look. That was *us*.

In life, spotting a poser is easy. A poser mimics the look and vibe of a group they admire but lacks any authentic connection to it. Take the guy decked out in basketball jerseys who's never set foot on a court or the woman who practically lives in Lululemon but has never touched a yoga mat. Posing is the act of trying to be something you're not to impress others. Here's a tip: just be yourself—it's always a better look.

My brother and I grew up middle-class in San Diego, the birthplace of skateboarding. We were raised by a hard-working mom who was a hairstylist and a dad who wore many hats: doughnut shop manager, substitute teacher, Huffy Bikes sales rep, and eventually a door salesman. We went to St. Columba, a small Catholic school in Serra Mesa, where cliques weren't a thing. With fewer than 30 kids per class, everyone hung out with everyone—nerds, sporty kids, and everyone in between. We wore uniforms, and even outside of school, no one dressed to impress. Life felt simple. For nine years, I assumed that's just how the world worked.

Then came high school.

The local high school, Serra High, had a reputation my parents weren't thrilled about—great for skating, not so much for academics. Lucky for me, my aunt taught math at a much better school in Scripps Ranch, a fancy neighborhood about ten minutes north. My parents worked some magic, and I found myself enrolling there instead.

I knew one person: my best friend from St. Columba, who happened to live in Scripps. That first week of initiation, I sat in the back of the gym bleachers, watching. The jocks and popular girls clustered together, band kids chatted exclusively among themselves, and theater kids laughed and joked in their own bubble. Everyone seemed to know their place—except me.

By the end of the first day, it was clear I needed to pick an identity, or one would be assigned to me. I gravitated toward sports and somehow landed in the "cool" crowd. But later that year, I found the skater group. They weren't concerned with fitting into anyone's expectations, and they introduced me to an important concept: posers. It didn't take long to realize that some of the "cool" kids I'd been hanging out with were the biggest posers of all.

High school is a jungle. At its core, it's about one thing: convincing your crush you're not a total loser. Everyone fakes it to some extent—and that's okay, as long as you don't fake it forever. Eventually, you have to put in the work.

Those of us who were teenagers in the '90s are a unique breed. We grew up playing outside, wandering the streets until dinner, yet we adapted to the rise of technology. Born in the late '70s and early '80s, we're part of a micro-generation: *Xennials*—a mix of Gen X and Millennials. We learned computers and the internet from Gen Xers who barely understood them. Case in point: the Y2K panic, when the world genuinely thought computers would self-destruct because they weren't programmed for the year 2000.

By my junior year, society's perception of skateboarders was shifting. What had once been the uniform of outcasts became edgy and desirable. Thrasher shirts went from underground to haute couture. Jocks who used to bully me for my tattered skate shoes were suddenly cruising on short cruisers, desperately trying to look the part. And, of course, they almost always pushed Mongo.

Music was central to skateboarding culture, and it shaped who I was. My Discman was a lifeline between classes, blasting *Bad Religion, NOFX, Blink-182,* and *Pennywise.* At the gates, my white Jeep Cherokee's 12-inch subs rattled mirrors with Biggie, 2Pac, Wu-Tang, and Nas. Back then, you didn't flex with Instagram followers; you earned respect by the CDs in your massive Jansport binder.

Music bridged the gap. Suddenly, the same girls who used to think skaters were weird found themselves vibing to our soundtracks. Skaters didn't seem so strange anymore.

As soon as the girls took notice, everything changed. Jocks, cheerleaders, and anyone chasing social currency started skating—or at least pretending to. And, unsurprisingly, the number of Mongo pushers skyrocketed. These kids weren't interested in the culture—they just wanted to look the part.

Posers

In high school, "poser" was the ultimate insult. Worse than being called a nerd, a rat, or even a jock. Quietly, I *was* a jock. I'd played sports my whole life, but with some finesse, I managed to float between cliques—a social chameleon of sorts. My lunch routine was a delicate balancing act.

I spent the first ten minutes of lunch with the jocks, who ruled the school from their self-proclaimed Mayan temple—a podium-shaped platform with six steps on each side. (Yes, I remember it was six, not five or seven, because I'm a skateboarder. The runway was too short to skate, but that didn't stop me from imagining what could've gone down that set.)

At the top of this temple were the most popular girls, their perfect smiles shining as they whipped their ponytails back and forth. The jocks orbited them on the lower steps, trying their best to attract a glance or a laugh—peacocks in full display. Some strutted more effectively than others. Meanwhile, the less cool guys (my people) played hacky sack at the base of the stairs. That's where I fit into the "cool" clique. We had no chance of competing with the peacocks, but honestly, we weren't trying to.

After ten minutes of social diplomacy, I'd make my escape—at great risk to my reputation—crossing the quad to the shaded corner where the skaters hung out. The skaters *hated* the cool kids, and they weren't shy about accusing me of being a poser. Me! A poser! Thankfully, after a few sessions, they realized I was the real deal, and I was welcomed in. They understood why I spent time with the cool kids: *the girls*.

To be fair, I didn't date much in high school. Skating came first. But I couldn't help daydreaming about someday having a girlfriend. Occasionally, being shy worked in my favor. Case in point: senior year. One of the flyest girls in school, Erica Overski, asked *me* to the Sadie Hawkins dance.

I was stunned. As a lower-tier member of the cool clique, I'd already resigned myself to staying home. Most of my friends had dates, and I figured I was out of luck. But then it happened. One glorious day in history class, Erica sat next to me—a rare occurrence. A few minutes later, she was called to the front of the room to show her work on the projector. As she turned it on, the words on her paper lit up: *"Brett, will you go to Sadie's with me?"*

Was it the most creative ask? Not really. But bold? Absolutely. Erica knew she didn't need a grand gesture—she was one of the coolest girls in school. And she knew there was no way I'd say no. The jocks in class were floored. Sure, most of the top-tier guys were already taken, but Erica could've gone alone. Instead, she chose a real skater. Fast-forward twenty years, and it's totally normal to see the hottest girls with skaters. *You're welcome, Nyjah.*

Looking back, I'd like to think Erica saw something in me I didn't fully realize at the time: authenticity. Being comfortable in your own skin, flaws and all, is an under-rated trait—and one that skateboarding has always championed. If you want to be a skateboarder, I say go for it. Get yourself a board, put in the work, and be real about it.

"But how do I start?" you might ask. Or, more importantly, "How do I avoid looking like a poser if I don't have any skills?" Great questions! Let's tackle the poser part first.

Spotting a Poser

It's not always easy to tell who's a poser just by looking at them. In skateboarding, your board is more than recreation—it's your identity. Someone can dress the part, ride a board, and still not *be* a skateboarder.

First, let's exclude longboarders. Most longboarders know exactly who they are. They're probably surfers at heart, carving up sidewalks like waves, grooving to their own rhythm. They're not posers—they're just doing their own thing. And for that, I respect them. After all, surfers created skateboarding back in the '50s when they wanted to bring the waves to the pavement. Hats off to those guys.

But here's the real secret: skateboarding has its own quirks, little markers that insiders pick up on. One of the most obvious? How someone pushes their board. If they push Mongo—with their front foot—they're almost certainly a poser.

Why is Mongo pushing so atrocious, you ask?

On the surface, pushing with your front foot seems

logical—until you realize how inefficient it is. I get it. When most people jump on a skateboard for the first time, their instinct is to place their dominant foot on the tail. Naturally, they use it to steer and balance while pushing with their other foot. It makes sense: your dominant foot does the heavy lifting, and your non-dominant foot follows suit.

Except it doesn't *feel* right. It's awkward. Unnatural. But you chalk it up to inexperience and power through, convinced there's no way you could use your less dominant foot to steer and balance while pushing. And so, onward you go—doomed from the start.

What every skateboarder eventually learns, either from watching idols or local park legends, is that real skaters push with their back foot. They steer and balance with the front, leaning left or right to weave through obstacles without ever stopping to realign. That fluidity—the ability to lean and carve with ease—is what sets skateboarders apart. Once you can push and ride confidently, chasing that smooth, exhilarating feeling becomes second nature. That's the moment you're no longer just someone who rides a board. You're a skateboarder.

Of course, getting there isn't easy. I know because I still struggle to switch things up when skating *switch stance*— riding with your less dominant foot in the back. Why would anyone put themselves through that kind of frustration, you ask? Simple: it makes you better. Think of it like kicking a soccer ball with your non-dominant foot. Sure, it's hard to learn, but it gives you an edge. It makes you a more versatile player, unpredictable on the field. (Shoutout to *Dembele* for keeping defenders guessing.)

The same principle applies to skateboarding. Skating switch broadens your skillset and opens the door to a new level of mastery. For example, every skater wants a clean **tre**

Land on Both Feet

flip *(short for three-sixty flip)* in their repertoire. It's not the easiest trick to learn, nor the hardest, but it's a classic. Josh Kalis had one of the best. If you see someone with a good *tre flip*, you know they've got serious talent. Now, if that same skater has an equally clean *switch* tre? Undeniable legend status.

For the record, I've landed a few *switch tres* in my life, and let's just say they weren't pretty. Picture someone trying to solve a calculus problem on a whiteboard while treading water. Yeah, that's me attempting a *switch tre*.

The key to skating switch—without falling into the dreaded Mongo trap—is learning to push with your other foot. *Pushing regular gives you more control, more speed, and the ability to transition smoothly into tricks.* Mongo pushing, on the other hand, throws off your balance and forces an extra body rotation to get into your stance. It slows you down and limits your options. Pushing regular means you're ready for action the moment your back foot leaves the ground.

From a skater's perspective, *pushing correctly is a rite of passage.*

I'VE LIVED IN NEW YORK ON AND OFF FOR ABOUT SEVEN YEARS, and I see people skating all the time. Watching someone walk around holding their board, it's tough to tell how experienced they are. Sure, there are a few subtle signs—like how they hold their board—but I won't spoil that secret. Gotta keep some things in the culture.

But the second that person steps on their board, it's game over. I can instantly tell how good they are by their push, their stance, the way they carry themselves. In that moment, I feel an unspoken connection to them, maybe even more than I feel with some of my closest friends. *It's not just about skateboarding—it's the way we think, react, and view the world.*

It's a rare and unique feeling, knowing so much about a stranger just by watching them ride.

More on that later.

Purpose

Underneath it all, pushing with your back foot isn't just about efficiency. It's not just about following the only unanimous unwritten rule of skateboarding, avoiding ridicule, or earning respect. *Pushing with your back foot is about purpose.*

It's easy to let life unfold passively. You follow the prescribed path: go to school, get good grades, make some friends, get into college, work a part-time job, graduate, embark on a career, start a family, and, if you're lucky, scrape together enough for a one-bedroom condo or a house with a picket fence. But for what? What's the point? Not *the* purpose of life, but *your* purpose—day in and day out. What do you want it to be?

Think about a goal you've set for yourself. It could be as big as buying a million-dollar house or as small as perfecting an ollie. The specifics don't matter, but the intent does. If your goal is that house, how do you get there? You probably don't know every step, but you know what not to do. Blowing money on things you don't need or drowning your paycheck at the bar isn't helping. You need a plan, discipline, and time. If you're serious about it, you can make it happen.

But everyone starts from a different place. Some

people are born into wealth and privilege, already halfway up the ladder. Others start at a much steeper incline. It's not fair, but that's the reality. Understanding where you're starting from is crucial because starting from the beginning isn't the same as starting from scratch. The beginning is relative—it's your personal starting line.

Take my dad, Big Al. On my ninth birthday, he promised me he'd quit smoking. And he did, cold turkey—until he didn't. More than 30 years later, he still smokes. Part of him probably wants to quit, but not enough to take action. If he truly wanted to stop, he'd have to start small—because for him, quitting cold turkey isn't starting from zero; it's starting from below zero.

The same principle applies to skateboarding. If your goal is to ollie a ten-stair but you've only mastered three, you don't skip straight to ten. You work your way up. Master the three-stair—ollie it 20 or 30 times until it feels second nature. Then move on to the four-stair, then the five, and so on. Each step builds your confidence and ability. When the day comes to attempt that ten-stair, you'll be not only physically prepared but also mentally ready to roll away from it.

This concept of starting from your true beginning applies to finding purpose, too. It's not something you stumble upon—it's something you work toward. Maybe your purpose lies in spirituality, service, or simply in being a better version of yourself. Wherever you're starting from, it begins with small, intentional actions.

For me, it started with something as mundane as making my bed. On the surface, it made my room look nicer. But it also kept our dogs from dirtying our white sheets (a color I didn't choose, by the way). More importantly, it set the tone for my day. A small, deliberate act gave me momentum to tackle the rest of my tasks.

When I met Carinda in 2016, that routine shifted. (Yes, we met on Tinder, and no, we didn't hook up on the first night.) At first, I adapted by making my side of the bed while she slept. Later, when we moved in together, my mornings started with making her coffee instead. It wasn't the same, but it became my new first task. Over time, that small act of care evolved into its own routine, one that still grounds me today.

The point is, *small, purposeful actions create momentum.* Without them, the whole routine can unravel. Skip making the bed once, and it's no big deal. Skip it a few more times, and soon you've abandoned the habit altogether. It's a slippery slope, but the reverse is also true: small, intentional actions can snowball into greater discipline, confidence, and purpose.

So, why is pushing with your back foot so important? Because it's about leading with your front—being balanced, grounded, and focused. When you push Mongo, you're steering with your back foot, leaving you off-balance, unfocused, and looking down. It's chaotic. But when you push correctly, you're stable. You look ahead, out at the world, not down at your feet. And once it's second nature, you don't think about it anymore—you just go.

Skateboarding teaches you to look forward, to navigate obstacles instinctively. Over time, this habit spills into the rest of your life. You walk differently, with your head up and your eyes ahead. You notice the flow of foot traffic, make eye contact with strangers, and recognize humanity instead of obstacles. Suddenly, the world isn't just a sea of faces—it's filled with individuals, each on their own path.

You also realize how much your posture, stride, and

Land on Both Feet

demeanor affect how others see you—and how you see yourself. Straighten your back, lead with your chest, and move with purpose. Confidence doesn't just come from within; it comes from how you carry yourself. And before you know it, self-improvement becomes a habit.

It all starts with one small, deliberate act. Whether it's making your bed, keeping your phone in your pocket, or perfecting your ollie, these tiny choices build into something greater.

Lead with your front foot. Walk out your door with purpose. Keep your head up—because that's where your life is going.

Push with your back foot, and let the rest come naturally.

"Skateboarding teaches you how to take a fall properly. That's one of the biggest life lessons you learn because you're going to fall every day." ~ **Paul Rodriguez**

2

The Balance of Hell and Harmony

F alling sucks. There's no way to sugarcoat it. You're going to eat shit, and you're going to eat it often. You'll get better at avoiding serious damage, but let's be clear: you're *not* the exception. You won't be the one skater in history who avoids slamming their head on the pavement. If you're just starting out, don't be an idiot— wear a helmet. Your knees and elbows will heal. Your head won't. Once you've accepted your fate, we can move on.

Balance is the most essential skill in skateboarding. Like anything worth doing, it's learned in stages. What fascinates me is how this journey unfolds. At first, just standing on a skateboard while it's stationary is a challenge. This type of balance is all about your toes and heels. How loose or tight your trucks are will dictate how much give and take your board allows. There's no right or wrong tightness— some skaters ride trucks so tight they barely turn, while others ride them loose enough to wobble at high speeds.

Most beginners start by standing on their board in the grass to keep the wheels from moving. This is where you learn the basics. Stand on the board and pay attention to how its movement affects your body. Lean to one side and see what happens. Use your body to counteract the lean. This is the first step in learning to balance.

When I was sixteen, my stepdad Lyle gave me his Jeep Cherokee. It was a 4x4 with a grill, off-road lights, and a modest lift—not one of those obnoxiously high lifts that scream "compensating." Right after I got my license, Lyle took me to a dirt and gravel parking lot to teach me how to drift.

The fun part was countersteering. When you're joyriding on slick trails, it's easy to lose control. The trick is to whip the wheel against the direction you're sliding to regain traction. When the car catches, it whips the other way—at which point you countersteer again. It's a constant back-and-forth, balancing the car's momentum. Learning to balance on a skateboard is similar. Through trial and error, you anticipate what the board needs and use your body to mediate the fall. Lean too far right, and you'll eventually need to lean left. It's a constant adjustment.

Once you've mastered standing on your board in the grass, the next step is rolling. This is where things get harder. Now you're balancing on two axes: toes and heels, front foot and back foot. At first, it feels impossible. Start small. Place one set of wheels in a sidewalk crack to keep the board from moving. Get comfortable. When you're ready, move to smooth cement and let gravity propel you forward.

The most common beginner falls happen when you slip forward or backward trying to counterbalance. Falling sideways? Not so bad—you can usually just step off. But if you're caught leaning too far forward or back, you'll hit the pavement in a second flat. And trust me, you'll learn to hate gravel—it's no fun picking little rocks out of your face.

One unavoidable enemy of every skater is wheelbite. That's when a stray pebble or crack stops your wheel dead, sending you flying. It's part of skateboarding. Don't let it discourage you—it happens to everyone.

Once you're rolling comfortably, you'll want to go faster. To go faster, you'll need to push. And yes, you push with your back foot. If you said front foot, start this book over.

Pushing introduces a new layer of complexity. When you lift your back foot to push, all your balance shifts to your front foot, which is placed parallel to the board. This is a whole different ballgame. Now you're balancing side-to-side *and* heel-to-toe, all on one foot. At first, it feels awkward. You'll have to get used to leaning on the sides of your foot to navigate. Over time, as you gain speed, momentum helps stabilize you.

It might take years to feel completely comfortable pushing, and that's okay. I've seen kids who look like they're fighting for their lives to stay balanced but still pull off a kickflip down a five-stair at the park. Skateboarding has a way of humbling and surprising you at the same time.

The key to learning balance—and skateboarding in general—is taking it step by step. Master the basics before you dive into tricks. Pushing, riding, and balancing are skills you'll use every time you step on your board. You'll practice them nonstop, whether you mean to or not.

Falling is inevitable, but every fall teaches you something. Balance isn't just a skill; it's a mindset. It's about constant adjustment, anticipation, and finding harmony in the chaos.

Keep at it. The pavement might win a few battles, but if you stick with it, you'll win the war.

MY FIRST TRICK WAS NOT AN OLLIE

Impact balance is your next hurdle in skateboarding. You can start practicing by doing squat jumps off your board: bend your knees, explode upward, and land on the balls of your feet, using your bent knees and core to absorb the impact. It's all about control. An ollie essentially uses the same concept—only you're doing it while balancing on the board. Yeah, not easy. I started learning to ollie in the grass, though I took an unexpected detour along the way.

I first decided I wanted a skateboard after seeing a kid at Tecolote Youth League in San Diego. (TEC ATTACK!) After baseball practice one day, I saw him pull his skateboard out, sit on it with his baseball bag in his lap, and ride down the hill from the field. It looked like pure fun. Watching in amazement, I couldn't resist asking him about his board. He let me try it out in the grass, and that was it. Challenge accepted.

At the time, my parents were divorced. Big Al—my dad —was the softie between the two, so naturally, I asked him first. Neither of us knew what made a good skateboard, so we ended up with a cheap one: plastic trucks, plastic wheels, and bearings that barely moved. But it didn't matter—I was stoked. That night, I headed to the backyard with my new board and set out to learn how to ollie.

For three hours, I practiced. I bent my knees, popped the tail, and dragged my front foot up the board, just like I'd seen in skate videos. Over and over, I tried. Nothing. The excitement of having my own skateboard kept me going for a while, but eventually, frustration set in. I kept losing my balance and couldn't get the timing right. Then, during one attempt, I accidentally kicked the tail sideways. The board spun 180 degrees beneath me, and when it landed, my back foot hit the ground, but my front foot stayed on the board.

Sick!

I had no idea what it was called (a Pop Shuvit)—but it was a trick. And even though I didn't land on both feet, it felt amazing. Much like Rodney Mullen's first accidental flip, it was as if the board were speaking to me, challenging me to figure out whatever the hell had just happened.

That moment was an epiphany. I vividly remember standing there, looking at the board like it had a life of its own. I started experimenting, trying to replicate the motion: popping the tail and making it spin. Forty or fifty tries later—well past my usual baseball practice bedtime—I landed it. My first trick. A pop shuvit.

Sure, I wasn't rolling. I could barely ride yet. But I'd done a trick. I jumped for joy, and I remember Big Al coming outside to check on me. I wonder if he realized then that he'd created a monster.

That first skateboard was so bad it couldn't even roll downhill properly. The next time I brought it to the baseball field, I sat on it, ready to mimic what I'd seen that kid do, only to find I actually *lost* speed going downhill. This wouldn't do.

Eventually, Big Al and I went to Play It Again Sports on Garnet Street in Pacific Beach. We traded in my cheap board for a used one with metal trucks and wheels that spun—though the bearings made an awful howl. I didn't care. All I knew was that it rolled, and it had potential. Compared to my Toys 'R' Us board, it was a masterpiece.

Now my skateboarding journey could truly begin.

Land on Both Feet

A Razor's Edge

As you progress in skateboarding, you'll eventually face the challenge of balancing on one set of wheels. Whether it's a manual or a grind trick on a single truck, this type of balance demands mastery of everything you've learned about balance so far. It's what I like to call *teeter balance*—the combination of side-to-side, heel-to-toe, and forward-backward balancing.

Teeter balance is primarily used in manual tricks. A manual is when you balance on your back or front two wheels while riding. To learn it, start by riding forward, then apply pressure to the tail while using both your front and back feet to stabilize—think of it like balancing on a seesaw. Your back leg should be relatively straight with a slight bend at the knee, while your front knee stays deeply bent to lift the front wheels just off the ground.

Technically, you could pop the board into a manual for a second and bring it back down, but that's not what we'd call a proper manual. A true manual involves holding the balance across a surface, no matter how short or long. In parking lots, for example, you'll often find small four- or five-foot-long sidewalks with curbs on either side that separate rows. We call these manual pads. The goal? Ollie onto the manual pad, hold the manual across the entire surface, and drop off cleanly on the other side.

A manual requires mastery of all three types of balance. There's the side-to-side and heel-to-toe axis on the approach, teeter balance during the manual itself, and impact balance when landing back on the board without bailing. Learning teeter balance while doing a manual is no easy feat if you haven't nailed the fundamentals. If you can't ollie consistently and land squarely on your board every time, go back and practice. You should be able to ollie blindfolded and stick the landing. The ollie should stop being just a trick and instead become a tool—a vehicle for doing other tricks.

Rodney Mullen, one of the most technical skaters of all time, made manuals an art form. Tricks like the *tre flip* nose manual nollie flip are prime examples of his mastery. The level of balance, precision, and control required to pull off something like that is insane.

Here's the thing: anyone can kickflip a ten stair if they have the guts to try. But balancing through a technical manual trick? That takes a different kind of skill, the kind that's *earned* through patience, practice, and relentless dedication. It's a level of mastery I've always admired.

The Hardest Trick of All

There's one more type of balance in skateboarding, often overlooked but essential for certain grind tricks: *pinch*. Pinching is used on grinds like crooked grinds and some variations of 5-0 grinds. It involves concentrating all your weight over a specific wheel while locking the opposing side of your deck onto the ledge or rail. This "lock-in" creates stability as you grind, combining precision and control.

Most grinds and slides rely on a combination of the two standard axes of balance: heel-to-toe and front-to-back. But for crooked grinds, it's all about the pinch. Your wheel grips on one side, your deck anchors on the other, and together they keep your truck grinding smoothly.

This brings me to what I believe is the hardest trick in skateboarding in terms of balance: the 5-0 grind on a round rail. Not a tweaked 5-0 or one where you sneak in some pinch to help—just a clean, perfectly balanced, metal-to-metal grind with no tail dragging. It's pure balance, and it's brutally unforgiving.

Pulling off a proper 5-0 grind is both thrilling and nerve-racking. Even the best pros can't consistently 5-0 a flat bar. The margin for error is razor-thin. And yet, it's a trick that's accessible to anyone willing to endure the challenge. You'll fall out of balance more times than you can count, but when everything lines up—when the stars align —it's magical.

I'll never forget landing a 5-0 on the nine rail at Beverly Hills High School. The first time I tried, I was too scared to commit fully, and the grind ended up slightly tweaked to the left. But I went back on another trip and did it right—a proper 5-0. That feeling was unparalleled. It was like the first day of summer vacation: pure freedom, pure joy.

There's something uniquely beautiful about a 5-0 on a flat bar. It's deceptively simple, yet endlessly satisfying. While every skater has their own style, a well-executed 5-0 looks strikingly similar across the board—a universal aesthetic. It's a trick that demands near-perfect balance. Your arms, your weight, everything falls into place as if by instinct.

Unlike some tricks where you can "sit" on it or rely on a lock-in, a true 5-0 grind is all about balance. It's fleeting. You can't settle into it. It's a moment of perfect harmony, a trick that strips skateboarding down to its purest form.

Learning it is hell. You'll slam, you'll overcorrect, you'll misjudge your approach. But when you finally get it, you'll understand why it's worth it. A proper 5-0 isn't just a trick —it's a testament to precision, control, and the sheer beauty of balance.

MAINTAINING BALANCE IS UP TO YOU

Balance, in any part of your life, is essential to living fully. But *finding* balance is anything but easy. Sometimes, it's doing the task you've been putting off for weeks. Other times, it's giving yourself permission to leave it for tomorrow. It might mean skipping a boys' night out to spend time with your family—or letting loose on a crazy night out because you need it. There's no universal blueprint for balance because everyone's life is different. Ultimately, only you can find yours.

Let's try something. Humor me for a moment. Take a bird's-eye view of your life. If you're sitting at a desk, imagine your life spread out in front of you. Is your desk messy? Clear it off—we need a blank slate. (If your desk looks like mine, this won't take long. I can't stand clutter, which probably doesn't surprise anyone who knows how much I obsess over making my bed perfectly.)

If you're at home, look at the wall in front of you. Imagine your life as a puzzle, with all the little pieces stuck up there. How do you see them? Are they scattered, waiting to be put together? Are some already connected? Are certain pieces bigger, maybe sticking out more than the rest?

I'll do the exercise with you:

- Skateboarding.
- Aro (my son).
- Cleo (my daughter).
- Carinda (my wife, who will probably give me hell for listing skateboarding first—but babe, it's a skateboarding book, take it easy).
- Work.
- Friends.

Land on Both Feet

- Restaurants.
- Travel.
- Parents.
- Golf.
- Adventure.
- Health.
- Road trips.
- Life goals.

As I visualize my life, I realize there are pieces I've forgotten: hiking, Tuesday night soccer. I miss those things —they deserve a place on the wall, too. Maybe you've noticed the same in your life.

The truth is, we all have too many puzzle pieces and never enough time. How do we make space for everything we love? How do we experience everything we want to experience? Here's the good news: there *is* time—if you allow yourself to search for it.

That said, I get it. There are times in life when time feels nonexistent—I've been there. As a film editor, I worked on a specific Netflix worldwide release (which shall remain nameless), where, for three weeks straight, I averaged 80 to 90 hours a week. My days started between 7:00 and 9:00 a.m. and ended anywhere from 11:00 p.m. to 3:00 a.m. I'd cab home, sleep, and do it all over again—for 21 straight days. The money was good, but it wasn't sustainable.

My brother Bryce, a chef in Manhattan, knows this grind all too well. His days often stretch to 16 hours if someone calls out or a party of 20 shows up demanding custom menu alterations. Add being a father of two into the mix, and his responsibilities are staggering. Yet, Bryce has more balance now than ever. He spends time with his family, plays golf a couple of times a month, and makes time for himself.

How? He learned to manage his time efficiently. When your time is truly limited, you start to prioritize. You take control.

Have you ever said, "I'd love to do that, but I just don't have time right now"? Try reframing it: "I'd love to do that, but I haven't made it a priority yet." *Same outcome, different message.* It shifts the responsibility onto you. There's power in acknowledging that.

For adults and kids alike, there's always time if you're willing to find it. You can wake up 30 minutes earlier to work out. Prep your lunch instead of buying it. Read a book or take a bike ride instead of scrolling on your phone. Even if life feels chaotic, it's within your control to carve out moments for what matters.

Here's the thing: finding balance doesn't happen overnight. Like marriage or mastering a 5-0 grind on a flat bar, it takes constant effort. And maintaining balance? That's even harder. Take it from someone who sometimes has to schedule time just to skateboard—despite having dedicated an entire book to it.

Start simple. Make a list of the things that make you happiest. Now, get a wall calendar—not an app, not Alexa. Handwrite your plans. Hang it somewhere you'll see it every day. Pencil in time for what you love—not just for this week, but for the next month or two. This visible, tactile reminder holds you accountable.

Even if your life is chaos, this practice will help keep your ship afloat. You might even find yourself adjusting over time—swapping out one activity for another that feels more pressing or fulfilling. That's the beauty of taking control: you're the one making those decisions.

The best things in life take work. Mastering your craft requires commitment. Living a fulfilling life demands balance. And landing a perfect 5-0 grind on a round flat bar? That takes harmony.

But you're a skateboarder—or at least, you're thinking like one now. You already know how to keep grinding through hell and back. The real challenge comes after you land: figuring out how to hold on.

～

"The biggest obstacle to creativity is breaking through the barrier of disbelief." ~ **Rodney Mullen**

3

We're Not Made of Glass

You're going to eat shit. Often. There's no way around it. Sure, you'll get better at avoiding serious injuries but brace yourself—you're going to slam your head (your *helmeted* head, because you're not an idiot, right?) on the pavement more than a few times.

Let's talk about falling. (Wait...didn't the last chapter already start with falling? Yup, sure did. Get used to it.) Falling is inevitable in skateboarding, and if you stick with it, you'll come to realize it's more than just an inconvenience—it's essential. Pain, as counterintuitive as it sounds, is your friend.

I know what you're thinking: *Who in their right mind likes pain?*

Believe me, I get it. Every time I take a hard slam, there's a moment where I wonder why I ever picked up a skateboard in the first place. But here's the thing: pain is part of the cycle.

A "slam" is what we call a hard fall. And slams are rarely graceful. Most of the time, they blindside you. You don't just bounce back up and dust yourself off like nothing happened. No, you lie there on the ground, throbbing, desperately trying to hold back tears (but let's be honest, you're crying).

I've had my fair share of slams, and unfortunately, some of the worst are immortalized on tape. My friends still get a kick out of replaying the footage. I'm looking at you, Bryan.

Okay, fine. I'll reopen this scab for your amusement—but you're going to have to wait until the end of the chapter. Trust me, it's worth it.

Slams aren't just a rite of passage; they're how you learn. Every time you fall, your body and brain make micro-adjustments. You subconsciously calculate how to better position yourself next time to avoid the same mistake. You learn how to fall in ways that minimize damage—rolling out, breaking your fall with your arms, or tucking your chin to protect your head.

It's a skill. And like any skill, it takes practice.

There's also a mental component. Falling forces you to confront fear. That gnawing hesitation before attempting a trick for the first time is universal. You're calculating the risk, imagining the worst-case scenario. And yet, you still go for it. That's skateboarding in a nutshell—facing your fears, slamming hard, and getting back up anyway.

Pain isn't just a teacher—it's a measure of your progress. Every bruise, scrape, and rolled ankle tells a story. They're badges of honor. Proof that you tried something new, pushed your limits, and grew because of it.

Skate Day

There's nothing in the world that brings me more joy than skating with my friends, which is why I love my birthday skate sessions. Sure, I skate as much as I can as a father of two, but my birthday is special—it's *my* skate day. Friends come out to show support, hang out, and skate together. It's easily the best day of the year.

I started the Birthday Challenge when I turned 33. That year, I decided to land 33 tricks in one day. Since then, my love for birthdays has leveled up. Unlike most people, I actually look forward to my birthday year-round. Sure, there's the gathering at a local bar, visiting family, and getting a free pass on chores, but the main event is the skate day. The goal? Land as many tricks as I am years old.

The rules are simple:

- No repeating tricks on different obstacles.
- Tricks must be of moderate difficulty—no low-effort passes.
- Everything has to be completed in a single calendar day.

My friend Bryan London has filmed most of my birthday skate days, just as I've filmed his. Bryan and I go way back—we met at YMCA Missile Skatepark. I was a camper fresh out of middle school, and he was a 15-year-old volunteer instructor. If you're a skater, his name might ring a bell: Bryan turned pro for Arcade Skateboards, traveled the world, and even had a part in *411 Video Magazine*. That should date us pretty well.

That week at camp, Bryan and I became best friends. From then on, we spent almost every weekend at each other's houses. He lived 40 minutes north of me in Rancho Bernardo, while I split my time between my parents' houses in Serra Mesa and Pacific Beach. Shoutout to our parents for driving us back and forth every weekend until we could drive ourselves.

Land on Both Feet

IN 2020, I SPENT A FEW MONTHS IN PHOENIX LEADING UP TO Carinda and my wedding on February 22. My birthday, February 10, landed just before the big day. Naturally, I assured Carinda that I wouldn't hurt myself during my skate day—I wasn't about to wheelie down the aisle or hobble through our first dance. She knows how important skate days are to me and (begrudgingly) accepted that there was no stopping me. I promised not to do anything stupid. Fortunately, I kept my word.

Every year, skate day gets harder. I don't know when or how I'll have to stop skating, but the thought alone kills me. Achieving my birthday skate goal becomes increasingly difficult with age. Logically, I know the formula could be reversed: fewer tricks as I get older. But let's face it—"20 tricks at 40" doesn't have the same ring as "40 at 40."

Turning 40 was a tough pill to swallow, but my 40th skate day was unforgettable. More on that in Chapter 10.

After my 36th skate day, I was wrecked. For two days straight, I could barely move. I had to *lift my leg with my arms* just to get into the tub. It felt like my body was giving up on me. The older I get, the harder skate days hit. Without proper training, recovery becomes a real struggle.

We're not made of glass, but we're not indestructible either. One of my biggest regrets is not embracing strength training when I was younger. Back in the '90s, lifting weights was for athletes who wanted to "get big," not for skateboarders. We were all skinny kids with huge calves from jumping all day.

Today, plenty of pro skaters incorporate strength training into their routines. Dashawn Jordan, for example, looks more like a linebacker than a skater—but his power and precision on a board are unmatched.

As a kid, I hated when adults would tell me, "You'll understand when you're older." Sure, they were right about some things, but here's the part they don't often admit: wisdom comes from making a ton of mistakes. Most of what I've learned has been through trial and error, not just by growing older.

Strength training could've prolonged my "youth" on a skateboard. It's not too late to start, though. Something I recently learned from a physical therapist: one hour of strength training adds three hours to your life. Do it long enough, and you can buy yourself a few years. Not bad, right?

Skate days remind me of why I fell in love with skateboarding in the first place: the community, the challenge, and the pure joy of landing a trick. Every birthday skate session is another reminder that while age might slow me down, it can't take away the passion.

The best things in life—skating, family, balance—all take work. Landing a 5-0 grind on a round flat bar demands perfect harmony. So does living a full life. It's about effort, perseverance, and learning how to hold on after the landing.

For now, I'll keep celebrating my skate days, grinding through the pain, and savoring every trick while I still can.

My First Slam

Taking slams as a teenager, I could bounce right back up, dust off, and keep skating a big set of stairs for hours. Now, falling feels different. The pain lingers. My tendons protest. Why does my arm hurt when I fell on my hip?

These days, a bad slam makes me think twice about trying the same trick again. But even now, I understand that falling is absolutely necessary.

The first slam of any skate day is where the real session begins—everything before that is just a warm-up.

Firsts are milestones, rites of passage burned into our memory. First kiss (*Erin Overbrockly*), first job (*Osiris*), first apartment (*San Diego State*). Ask me about almost anything, and I can remember my first.

My first bad slam is etched into my brain.

It happened on flat ground, but speed was the culprit. I was trying to ollie a grass gap—a patch of grass about four feet wide between two driveways. At the time, it was the longest gap I'd ever tried. The setup was simple but required precision: push as hard as I could down the sidewalk, swerve into the driveway to line up, ollie the gap, land, and swerve back onto the sidewalk. A lot of things had to go right for me to pull it off.

I bailed a few times to test the speed. Bailing, for the uninitiated, is trying a trick but not committing to land on the board. I needed as much speed as possible because, back then, I could only ollie so high.

Then came the moment: I decided to go for it. I pushed as hard as my scrawny legs could manage, lined up the ollie, and... the board shot out from under me, skidding into the street as I slipped backward onto the cement.

Damn.

I hopped up, grabbed my board, and told myself, *You got this. Just go faster, pop higher, and keep your center of gravity over the board.*

This time, I was ready. Across the street, Bryan was filming with my parents' old beta camera. I took off down the sidewalk, pushing harder than before, swerved into the driveway, crouched low, and popped the ollie. Midair, I felt it: *This is the one.*

Expecting to roll away, I landed with both feet planted on the ground.

Then—

SLAM!

Before I could blink, I was sprawled on the pavement. My back arm whipped through the air like a slingshot and hit the ground with a *SMACK!* The sound was so loud it probably echoed into the 7-Eleven parking lot a quarter mile away. The rest of my body skidded across the cement, shredding skin like grated cheese.

I don't remember much, but I'm pretty sure I cried like a baby. The pain was unlike anything I'd experienced. It was the shock that got me—the speed, the impact, the sudden realization of *what just happened?*

When I finally stopped hyperventilating, I checked my arm and leg. Scraped raw. Blood bubbled through layers of exposed skin. It was destined to be quite the trophy gash.

As I replayed the moment in my head, I realized my back wheel hadn't cleared the gap. It landed right between the edge of the grass and the cement. One inch farther, and I would've rolled away. One inch shorter, and I might've hit the grass and softened the blow.

I didn't get back up to try again. In fact, I debated whether I wanted to try skateboarding *at all* anymore. Was it really worth this much pain? I was traumatized.

Eventually, I rose from the dead. I dusted off my legs and arms as best I could without smearing blood everywhere. There was only one destination: home.

The gap was about a half mile from my house, and that first block was brutal. My legs shook with every step. I wiped the dried tears from my face, determined to pull myself together in case I ran into anyone I knew near the 7-Eleven.

By the time I got home, the pain had dulled. It wasn't as bad as I thought. I told my mom, *It's no big deal.* (If she ever saw the tape, she'd know otherwise.)

Sure, I wore gauze pads on my arm and leg for a week or two, but that was it. An hour earlier, it felt like the end of the world. An hour later, I was walking fine. I probably took the rest of the day off skating, but I felt... okay. I was alive.

Looking back, that first slam was a turning point. It taught me that pain is temporary. Fear fades. And even when you're scraped raw and doubting yourself, you're tougher than you think.

Skateboarding is full of moments like that. Moments where you're convinced you can't go on, only to find yourself back on your feet, board in hand, ready to try again.

That's the thing about slams—they hurt like hell, but they remind you that you're not made of glass.

You're a skateboarder. You'll survive. The truth is, the pain of falling fades, but the rush of finally nailing a trick sticks with you forever.

Never Skate Two Churches in One Day

That fall changed my life. Afterward, I approached flat gaps with much more caution. Years later, after I'd improved my skating, I went back to ollie that same gap—out of pure spite. But flat gaps were no longer the obstacles I sought out. Still, I learned something important from that slam: I was tougher than I thought. Sure, bones can break, and skin can bleed, but we heal.

Healing is a strange, beautiful process. It gives you time to reflect, whether you want to or not. And speaking of healing, it's time to rip the proverbial band-aid off and tell the *Oink story*.

It was a Saturday morning, and I was a teenager about three years into skateboarding. Bryan had spent the night at my dad's house in Pacific Beach. I had bleached blond hair, baggy basketball shorts, and an oversized T-shirt—a classic look that, honestly, hasn't changed much for me.

Our first stop of the day was a church a couple of miles away. The church had a multi-level parking lot with small brick walls separating the levels. One of the drops was over my head—taller than five-foot-nine. Naturally, it caught my eye.

Before committing, I jumped off the top to gauge the impact. It was... a lot. But after psyching myself up, I went for it. The first two tries, I bailed mid-air. Then, on the third attempt, I popped the ollie and rode away clean. Easy. I pumped my fist in the air, exhilarated.

High off the success, I decided to push my luck and try a 180. Bryan was stoked that I was even considering it, so I gave it a shot. After a couple of bails, I knew I wanted it. If I could land a 180 here, it'd open the door to bigger stair sets and, one day, even rails.

I committed on the next try. I popped, rotated, and descended. Mid-air, I felt the board slipping out from under my feet, but I thought I could stick it.

Then—

SLAM!

Pain exploded in my left foot like a firework. It shot up my leg, through my spine, and out of my mouth in a squeal that could only be described as... pig-like. *Oink.*

Bryan burst out laughing. Not at the slam itself but at the absurd noises I was making. In the moment, I was furious—and in a lot of pain. Looking back? Yeah, it's funny. A little ridiculous, even.

I didn't want to ruin the day, so we headed up to Rancho Bernardo as planned. The plan was to crash at Bryan's house and skate again on Sunday. My naïve teenage brain figured a little ice and a good night's sleep would do the trick.

Our second stop of the day was another church with a three-flat-three set of stairs. Bryan started skating while I hobbled around, barely able to put weight on my foot. Before I even got the camera out, Bryan had already landed a kickflip. That's the kind of skater he was—always ahead of the camera.

After getting a few kickflips on tape, Bryan decided to up the ante: a frontside flip. On one of his attempts, he slid out on the landing and slammed hard. He got up calmly and said, "I broke my arm."

I didn't even notice at first. Then I looked closer. His wrist was bent completely sideways.

Bryan didn't scream, yell, or make a sound. He just stated it matter-of-factly. I hated him for that because it made me look like an absolute wuss.

We both ended up at the hospital. Since I was there, I figured I'd get my foot checked out. Sure enough, I'd broken my first bone: a hairline fracture on one of my metatarsals. Bryan's arm, on the other hand, was completely wrecked.

We'd broken bones on the same day. At two different churches. Was God trying to tell us something?

To make matters worse, we were scheduled to go on a cruise with Bryan's mom the following week. We must've been quite the sight—me in a boot and Bryan with a full arm cast.

The doctor told me to stay off my skateboard for six

weeks: three weeks on crutches, three weeks in the boot, then a reevaluation. Six weeks felt like an eternity.

Naturally, I ignored the doctor's orders. I was back on my board in less than a month. Being told not to skate felt like being told not to live.

These days, six weeks without skating is a regular occurrence. I'm not thrilled about it, but between work, family, and keeping up with my daughter's first months of life, skating has temporarily taken a lower spot on the totem pole. Sleep and sanity have catapulted to the top.

That day taught me two things:

1. Never skate two churches in one day.
2. Our bodies are resilient, but they're not indestructible.

Healing takes time—physically and emotionally. But if there's one thing skateboarding has taught me, it's that we're tougher than we think. We take the slams, we endure the pain, and we get back up.

Eventually.

Pain and Progress

Those four weeks were brutal. I spent every day fantasizing about the moment I could ride again. My TV/VCR combo got a workout as I cycled through my collection of skate videos: Plan B, Birdhouse—you name it. I knew every trick, every line, every clip like the back of my hand. If the devil had offered me a deal—five years off the end of my life in exchange for skating again immediately—I might've signed on the dotted line. (Thank God I didn't.)

At the time, I couldn't see the lesson through the

misery. I was shackled to my boot, trapped in my own self-pity, and convinced my skateboarding days were over. My teenage brain, fueled by Sum 41's emo lyrics, ignored the doctor's confident reassurances. What if I *never* healed?

But I did heal. And fast. I realized that I wasn't made of glass—something painfully obvious now, but revolutionary back then.

Here's the thing: pain isn't your enemy. Pain is your friend. I know how ridiculous that sounds, but stick with me.

In skateboarding, pain is a currency of failure. If you're attempting a trick you've mastered on flat ground, the odds of falling—and hurting yourself—are slim. But take that same trick to a ten-stair, and the stakes rise exponentially. The risk of injury climbs with the difficulty and height of the challenge. In other words: no pain, no gain.

If pain is the yin, progress is the yang. A skateboarder's purpose is progression: to be better than you were yesterday. Yes, we compete against others for sponsorships or contests, but skateboarding is ultimately a battle with yourself. That's why it's so rewarding.

Progression is measured in two ways: **consistency** and **difficulty**.

Say you land your first *tre flip*. For a skater, that's monumental. You'll want to send it to your friends, post it online —show the world. But here's the catch: landing it once doesn't mean much if you can't do it again. Consistency takes time, sometimes years, to develop.

A great way to build consistency is through S.K.A.T.E.— a skateboarding version of H.O.R.S.E. in basketball. If you land a trick, your opponent has to match it. The more consistent your tricks, the better your odds of winning.

Then there's difficulty. This is where most skaters focus.

Once you've mastered a trick, the next logical step is to try it over a bigger or harder obstacle. That's where the idea of "hammers" comes in—those jaw-dropping tricks that close out skate videos and leave viewers in awe.

The Hammer That Broke Me

When I was 17, I was filming my first skate video part for K-5 Skate Shop in San Diego. I wanted a hammer to close it out—something that would leave people impressed.

The trick? A boardslide down an 11-stair handrail at a Catholic school. (Funny how my worst injuries always seem to happen at churches.)

I'd already boardslid a nine-stair rail, so two extra stairs didn't seem like a big leap. But this rail was intimidating—steep, tall, and perched on the second story of the school, with a huge drop on the opposite side.

It was sunset. My friend Dustin was filming, and the light was fading fast. I knew it was now or never.

When you're scared of a trick, you tend to go faster than necessary to ensure you clear the obstacle. That's exactly what I did. I popped the ollie, but instead of landing on the rail, I cleared it entirely.

Mid-air, I realized I had to bail. My weight was pitched forward, and there was no way to land safely. It was like committing to a belly flop and trying to avoid it at the last second. Impossible.

I landed on my feet, but the impact broke a few bones in my right foot. The pain was sharp, but I didn't cry or make a sound. Silver lining: there was no embarrassing footage of me whining. Mentally, I wasn't ready for that trick. The fear got the better of me, and it cost me.

Pain keeps us in check. It reminds us of our limits and teaches us to respect them. Pain isn't just a byproduct of failure—it's a sign of bravery. Fluke accidents aside, if you're hurting, it means you were pushing yourself. It means you had the courage to try.

Someone once said, "You can't steal second base with your foot still on first." For years, I had that quote framed on my bedroom wall. It perfectly encapsulates skateboarding.

Through enough slams and setbacks, pain becomes part of the process. You learn to assess risks, judge obstacles, and decide if the potential reward outweighs the cost. Over time, it becomes second nature.

Fail Like You Meant It

Failure is inevitable. It's also invaluable.

When you fall, you get back up. You try again. And again. And again. Skateboarders fail more often than they succeed, but that's the point. It's what separates us. We don't see failure as an endpoint—it's just another step toward progress.

To land your first kickflip, you might fail a thousand times. That's 999 failures before success. But skateboarding teaches you to embrace the grind. Instead of "failing," we call it "trying." Same result, different mindset.

This mental toughness is an incredible advantage in life. Skateboarding rewires your brain to see failure as a stepping stone, not a setback. Pain doesn't deter us—it motivates us.

We're not made of glass. We bruise, we bleed, we break —but we heal. Pain doesn't mean we're fragile. It means we're alive, growing, learning.

Every slam, every scrape, every broken bone is proof of our resilience. Yes, we fall—but we never stay down.

Keep pushing. Keep failing. Keep progressing.

And when you land that trick you've been chasing? It'll all be worth it.

$\sim$

"Skateboarding has no rules. You can create whatever you want out of it." ~ **Nyjah Huston**

4

When One Door Closes, Grind the Steps

You know what also sucks besides falling? Things coming to an end. The last day of summer, that dreaded Sunday before school starts, is the worst. Watching the credits roll after the final episode of *Schitt's Creek*? Awful. And don't get me started on Carl's Jr. discontinuing their French Toast Dips in 2010—I almost cried. I wish I could take credit for their glorious return five years later, but whoever made that happen, I owe you forever.

Approaching my teenage years, I started to grow frustrated with team sports. Baseball and soccer dominated most of my free time. I also dabbled in golf, football, and basketball. But let's be real—my grade school nickname was "Shorty," so basketball wasn't exactly my calling. My parents didn't shove sports down my throat, but they gave me a gentle nudge into the deep end. I didn't need much convincing.

Side note: I firmly believe every kid should have to play on a sports team in grade school, and every adult should be required to wait tables or bartend for at least one year. The world would be so much kinder.

When I picked up skateboarding, though, everything shifted. For the first time, I had something that was entirely my own. I loved playing sports, but I *lived* for skateboarding. Especially when it led me to explore.

The progression of skateboarding is like leveling up in a video game.

First, you learn to balance and ride, probably in front of your house. If your street has smooth asphalt or sidewalks, consider yourself lucky. Then you start learning to push with your back foot (*ahem, you know better by now*).

Once you've got pushing down, it's time for the ollie. It might take weeks—or months—but when you finally nail it, everything changes. Suddenly, you're testing it out on curbs. Then you venture out a little farther. You're competent enough to ride down the sidewalk without eating pavement too often, though it still happens. Hopefully, no one's around to see it.

Next, you hit up the local parking lot, ideally one with plenty of curbs. This is your first *real* practice space. You get comfortable ollieing and, eventually, start feeling the itch to explore. That's when the big leap happens: the skatepark.

In the beginning, your parents take you to the park early so you can roll around without getting in anyone's way. You learn skatepark etiquette—don't stand in the middle of the bowl, watch out for others, respect your fellow skaters. You figure it out quickly.

Soon, you're dropping in on quarter pipes and landing a few basic tricks. Maybe you've got a rocket kickflip or an ollie down a three-stair. By now, you've probably made some skater friends, either at the park or through school. Skateboarding becomes all-consuming. You race through homework just to get outside and onto your board.

If you're lucky, you convince your parents to build a fun box in your backyard. And if the yard isn't big enough? Just casually suggest they cement over that patch of grass they're always complaining about. "It'll save so much work in the long run!" (Big smile. It works. Thanks, Mom and Dad.)

After a long day of skating, you spend hours watching videos on YouTube or scrolling Instagram. That's when you notice something: while skateparks make plenty of appearances, the best clips—your favorite skaters' clips—are filmed in the streets.

The idea of street skating starts to take hold.

The discovery phase of skateboarding is intoxicating. It's like finding your first cheat code in a video game or experiencing your first kiss. Your mind explodes: *This is what everyone's been talking about!*

And once you're hooked? There's no going back.

The New Frontier

Once I started seeing the world through a skater's lens, everything changed. Buildings, parking lots, and alleys transformed. 7-Eleven wasn't just a post-school Slurpee stop anymore—it had a perfect manual pad tucked around the back. The park where we used to shoot hoops became an ideal flatground spot with bike racks to grind. Even the church down the street, where I'd spent years in Catholic school, now called to me with its enticing two-block.

Schools, businesses, parks, churches, parking lots, and strip malls—these became our treasure troves. We scoured every inch of the neighborhoods within a mile radius of our houses, turning ordinary places into playgrounds. Those early days were some of the best.

On weekends, we'd wake up early, pack our cameras, double-check the batteries, and head out. There was no time for breakfast—we'd hit Krispy's Doughnuts for a cinnamon roll or apple fritter to fuel up, warm up in the parking lot, and plot the day's route.

We were explorers charting unfamiliar territory. Finding new spots was as exhilarating as skating them. Stairs, gaps, ledges—anything that looked skateable was fair game. Our mental catalogs filled with spot locations. Even now, I could tell you where all the best stair sets and ledges were in our neighborhoods.

As we progressed, though, our local spots began to feel small, their magic fading with repetition. The urge to venture farther took over. Beyond our mile radius lay uncharted territory, a new frontier.

One day, I proposed a spot-searching expedition. About a mile from my mom's house in Serra Mesa, there was a police station, and just beyond that, a steep hill on Aero Drive that descended toward I-15. At the base of the hill, a smaller street veered sharply uphill. None of us had ever explored that far.

There were no guarantees—no promise of a perfect gap or hidden ledge—but the unknown was calling.

We set out early, our backpacks heavy with cameras, batteries, and Gatorades. After pushing past the familiar spots—7-Eleven, my infamous flat gap, the business parks —we reached the police station. From there, it was a fast, thrilling ride down the hill, though it got too steep to skate the last stretch. We walked the final quarter-mile to the base of the climb.

The hill loomed large in front of us. Shoulders aching, lungs burning, we powered through. As we neared the top, another building emerged over the horizon. Butterflies swirled in my stomach. I couldn't wait to see what lay ahead.

When we reached the summit, the world seemed to stop.

There, stretching out in every direction, were endless rows of business parks. Stairs, ledges, railings, parking lots —it was the holy grail.

For hours, we roamed the streets, discovering one spot after another. We didn't even skate much that day—the thrill of exploration was overwhelming. Mental snapshots of every ledge, gap, and rail filled my mind, replaying as we made the long trek home.

This stretch of business parks became our domain. The place where nine-to-fivers spent their weekdays dragging their feet was heaven for us on weekends. This was our land.

The Game Changer

As our explorations expanded, so did our reach. We mapped out every street in Pacific Beach, Bryan's neighborhood, and the surrounding areas. Each day was a mission, a chance to uncover something new.

But then everything changed: our friend Rob got a car.

Suddenly, the boundaries of our legs no longer dictated the scope of our adventures. With a car, the entire city opened up. We could spend our energy skating instead of trekking, exploring farther than we'd ever imagined.

Those days of driving through unfamiliar neighborhoods, scanning the streets for spots, were pure magic. The anticipation of discovering a perfect rail or ledge was almost better than skating it.

Even now, the thrill of discovery hasn't left me.

In the summer of 2022, just a few weeks after moving to Austin, I was walking my dogs past the local elementary school. There it was: a slightly downhill manual pad, perfect in every way. The first thing I noticed? Not the school, not the playground, but the spot. Some things never change.

Think Beyond Expectations

In Rancho Bernardo, there was a spot that felt like it was made for skateboarding: Webb Park. Today, you wouldn't even recognize it—all the stair sets, ledges, gaps, and walls have been transformed or removed. But back then, it was paradise for skaters.

The first time I spent the night at Bryan's, he took me to Webb Park and introduced me to his local crew. I was skating the three-stair when Bryan, Falco, and Justin started dragging one of the heavy cement benches toward the two-stair. They positioned the top of the bench on the first stair and the bottom on the landing, creating a ledge with a slight decline perfect for tricks.

I was blown away. I'd never thought about moving objects to create a new obstacle. It was brilliant, and watching them take turns hitting the makeshift ledge was mesmerizing. These weren't pros or anything (yet)—just regular skater kids using their creativity. Sure, I'd seen insane tricks in skate videos, but witnessing this kind of innovation firsthand shifted how I saw skateboarding entirely.

That day, something clicked. Skateboarding wasn't just about performing tricks on what was available—it was about creating something new.

Just around the corner was a Vons grocery store. Behind

it was a loading dock for deliveries, but for us, it was a gold-mine. The dock had a decent drop to skate off and a small metal-tipped ledge perfect for grinding or sliding. Sometimes we'd even use it as a manual pad to drop off the dock. It became our go-to warm-up spot in Bryan's neighborhood —a reliable start to any skate session.

One day, we realized the loading dock had even more potential. Grocery stores come with shopping cart racks, those heavy metal bays designed to corral carts. We decided to take one and position it at the edge of the dock, creating something similar to a handrail down a stair set. It wasn't perfect, but it worked.

That Vons loading dock became the first spot where I learned to boardslide a rail. Skating something we had envisioned and built ourselves was an incredibly satisfying feeling. It wasn't just a trick or a spot anymore—it was an extension of our creativity.

Those early days of finding and shaping spots taught me to see potential in places others overlooked. Webb Park and that loading dock weren't just skate spots—they were proof that skateboarding is as much about imagination as it is about skill.

Bust Factor

When I got my first car, I felt unstoppable. I drove everywhere, hunting for skate spots on my own or with friends. Once we exhausted every spot in San Diego, we expanded our horizons, taking day trips up to Anaheim and L.A. Those trips were legendary. We'd wake up at five in the morning, hit the road, and by sunrise, we'd be at UC Irvine, home to a perfect six-stair handrail.

If we were lucky, we'd skate there for a few hours

without any trouble. By eight, we'd usually all have landed a clip and still have the whole day ahead of us. From there, we'd make our way through Tustin, Laguna Hills, and Long Beach, always on the lookout for new spots. Lunch was almost always at a local taco shop. While Cali Burritos were a San Diego specialty, we found plenty of hidden gems in the greater L.A. area. I lived off rolled tacos smothered in melted cheese and guacamole—no sour cream, though. That stuff is gross.

A few trips later, we upped our game. We brought a generator and lights, which meant we could skate after dark. On those nights, we wouldn't head back to San Diego until 3 a.m. No matter how far we went, we always drove home the same day—hotels were out of the question for a crew as cheap as ours.

Because these trips were such a commitment, we knew we couldn't afford to waste opportunities. The spots we hit took time, effort, and planning, and some of them were one-and-done scenarios. Sometimes, the inevitable happened: we got kicked out.

Getting the boot always sucked, but it was part of the game. That's where our "bust factor" system came in. Every spot was rated on a scale from one to ten: one meant you could skate there almost anytime, while ten meant you'd never get more than a single try before getting chased off. Public parks were usually ones. Government buildings with security guards? Always tens.

Whittier College had the perfect nine-stair rail. It was square, not too high or low, and had a flawless runway and landing—no cracks in the pavement, nothing to throw you off. The first time we went there, we didn't even get to warm up before we got kicked out. That rail was so perfect I couldn't stop thinking about it. For weeks, I dreamt of skating it.

On our next trip to L.A., we strategized. We warmed up at a spot around the corner and showed up ready to go. Camera rolling, fisheye lens on, we parked the car and started throwing down on the rail immediately, expecting the boot was coming soon.

Every attempt felt like it could be our last. We skated like we were racing against the clock—because we were. Front board, smith grind, 5–0, lip slide, nose grind—one by one, we racked up tricks. David, Boris, Tyler, and I all landed multiple clips before we finally got kicked out, nearly an hour into the session.

There were still tricks I wanted to try, but we were pumped on the footage we'd gotten. That's the thrill of skating a high-bust-factor spot: sometimes the window closes before you land what you're chasing, and you have to accept it. But when you nail a difficult trick at a spot everyone knows is hard to skate, it earns you a level of respect only skaters understand.

It's that balance between risk and reward that makes skateboarding so unique. You're not just battling yourself—you're up against time, security guards, and the odds. And when it all comes together, it's worth every ounce of effort.

Chase the Horizon

As much as I thrived on adrenaline-fueled sessions at high-bust-factor spots, my favorite sessions happened at spots where we could just relax, experiment, and create. The best one we ever found was behind a warehouse in Mira Mesa. It quickly became known among our crew as the *setup spot*.

This place was a skater's dream: piles of wooden pallets, metal sheets, barrels, and random materials scattered everywhere. It became our first DIY skate spot—before DIY skate spots were even a thing. We built makeshift flat ramps leading up to ledges, stacked pallets to create grindable elevated platforms, and fashioned bumps over barrels. There was even a six-stair, a gap, and a handrail already in place around the corner.

It was the perfect blank canvas.

One afternoon, after countless sessions behind the warehouse, something changed. We started wondering what kind of business this place actually was. With all these materials lying around, it felt like it had to be something interesting. Boris, always the curious one, walked up to the back door and gave the knob a turn, fully expecting it to be locked.

It wasn't.

When the door creaked open, we hesitated, exchanging glances that silently asked, *Are we really doing this?* The answer was obvious. We stepped inside, flipped on the lights, and froze in awe.

It was a workshop.

There were metal benches, a truck with a metal-tipped flatbed, and an array of obstacles that seemed custom-designed for skating. And the floors—smooth as butter.

We skated until two in the morning, filming every trick we could muster. When our legs finally gave out, we put everything back exactly as we found it, hoping whoever worked there wouldn't notice we'd been there.

The next weekend, we returned. The door was unlocked again. Our secret gold mine, ready and waiting. For two nights straight, we skated until exhaustion, filming more tricks and reveling in our newfound treasure.

By Sunday, it felt like we had stumbled upon a hidden paradise, untouched by any other skaters. It was ours alone, a perfect convergence of chance and opportunity.

But, of course, it didn't last.

The next weekend, the door was locked. New security cameras had been installed outside. Someone had discovered our late-night escapades. While we could still skate the original setup spot out back, it just wasn't the same. Once you've tasted the filet, the strip doesn't quite hit the same.

I often think about that place, and not just for the skating. It was the feeling of seizing an opportunity, of pushing the limits of what was available to us. Those nights at the workshop were a reminder that sometimes, the most fleeting moments can leave the most lasting impressions.

I'm sure you've heard the quote from Alexander Graham Bell: *"When one door closes, another opens."* It's one of those sayings that gets tossed around in times of disappointment, meant to reassure us that something better is on the horizon.

But until recently, I didn't know that's only half the quote. The full version is: *"When one door closes, another opens; but we often look so long and so regretfully upon the closed door that we do not see the one which has opened for us."*

It hits differently when you hear the whole thing. The abridged version tells you not to worry—that opportunities will naturally come your way. But the full quote adds a layer of agency. It says: Stop staring at what's lost. Shift your focus, and you'll find the new path waiting for you.

Skateboarding taught me a similar lesson. Drawing from Bell's words, I came up with a simple expression that feels true to my experiences:

When a door closes, grind the steps.

Those nights at the warehouse, I didn't realize it at the time, but I was grinding the steps—making the most of what I had, refusing to let the opportunity pass.

It's easy to keep going when everything's falling into place, when life feels like a tailwind. But when the golden ticket disappears, when that perfect door slams shut, that's when the real test begins.

That's when you have to dig deep. Find the cracks others can't see. Create your own opportunities.

When a door closes, don't waste time lamenting what's lost. Find another way forward. Explore uncharted paths. Push through the unknown.

Keep grinding the steps, and you'll find out where they lead.

5

Respecting the Law Doesn't Mean You Shouldn't Break It

Street skating is skateboarding's purest form. Sure, skate parks and ramps are fun, but out in the streets —hanging with your friends, hunting for spots, and testing your limits—is where the soul of skateboarding thrives. Without this element, you're missing the most rewarding part of the culture: going out and creating something from nothing.

Sooner or later, every street skater runs into the same situation. It goes something like this:

You and your friends spot a five-stair on the way home from school. Maybe you've walked past it before, but today, you *really* see it for the first time. It's in a quiet business park, only a few blocks from your house. Perfect.

Within minutes of skating, the door to the print shop next to the stairs swings open. A middle-aged woman steps out, glaring. "There's no skateboarding here!" she barks. "It's private property. Leave now, or I'll call the cops!"

She slams the door.

You glance at your friends, a mix of confusion and frustration on everyone's face. There aren't any signs that say skating isn't allowed, but the last thing you want is for the cops to actually show up. So, you leave.

Still, you can't stop thinking about that perfect five-stair. Knowing you're *not* supposed to skate it only makes you want to skate it more. Later that day, back in your backyard, your usual fun box setup feels dull. That five-stair keeps creeping into your thoughts.

Finally, it hits you: Why not go back after the print shop closes? No Karen, no problem.

The next day, you and your crew scout out the spot after school. The sign on the door says the shop closes at six. Perfect. To kill time, you skate the curbs at the 7-Eleven down the street, realizing that no one there seems to care what you're doing—even though you're arguably in the way of cars pulling in and out.

Life doesn't always make sense, you're starting to realize. You just learn to roll with it.

At exactly six o'clock, you watch Karen lock up, get in her oversized Ford Expedition, and drive off, still talking loudly on her Bluetooth earpiece. It's time.

You and your friends descend on the five-stair, your boards echoing through the empty business park. The adrenaline rush is electric. You each take turns filming tricks on your iPhones, hyping each other up. Ollies are the move of the day—simple, clean, and confidence-boosting. One of you tries a 180 but bails, laughing it off.

For the next thirty minutes, it's just you, your crew, and the thrill of skating a "forbidden" spot. It's your first taste of real street skating, and it feels amazing. By the time you pack up and head home, you're already thinking about when you can come back.

The thing is, street skating isn't about defiance for its own sake. It's about creativity and freedom, about making something beautiful in a world that wasn't designed for it. Sure, you bent the rules, but no one got hurt. No property was damaged. And, most importantly, you took your skating to the next level.

Street skating doesn't mean you have to be reckless. Respect the spots, clean up after yourself, and don't leave a mess behind. But don't let anyone tell you that you can't chase the thrill of pushing boundaries.

Because sometimes, the "wrong" thing is the right thing for your soul.

To Run or Not To Run

Finding spots to street skate becomes increasingly challenging as you level up your skills. The five-stair sets in your neighborhood are great, but there are only so many smooth twelve-stair rails with clean runways. And when those prime spots happen to be heavily monitored, you're left with a decision: do you risk it, or let it go?

This is where skateboarding crosses into the gray area of legality. Skating on private property is technically a crime, even if there aren't any anti-skateboarding signs posted. More often than not, though, it's not the police you'll have to deal with. It's the Karens of the world, or power-tripping security guards, who make things complicated.

I grew up in San Diego—a middle-class White dude skating in a city that's a skater's dream. I've been privileged in many ways, including how I've been treated by authority figures during my teenage years. Still, the relationship between skaters and law enforcement has always been...complicated.

From my experience, most cops don't want to deal with

skateboarders. It's a waste of their time. But they'll respond if someone calls it in. Once in a while, though, you run into a cop who gets off on making an example out of you.

One weekend, I was skating at Serra High School—a legendary spot in '90s San Diego. The pros skated there. On this particular day, there were about ten of us, spread across the campus. I was mid-line, attempting a kickflip with the intention of completing a three trick line with a nosegrind. After botching the kickflip, I heard a yell from across the school:

"COPS! 5-0 5-0!"

We froze. Then, like clockwork, everyone grabbed their gear and bolted.

The cops sped into the parking lot like they were breaking up a bank heist. I ran instinctively, cutting through the fields at the back of the school. But these weren't amateurs—they had anticipated our move and circled around to cut us off.

Some kids were faster and got away. I wasn't. I doubled back, jumped a ten-foot metal fence with my backpack full of camera gear, and skated into a nearby strip mall to lay low.

Later, we regrouped at a spot we called the rendezvous six-stair, comparing stories. Some had gotten away; others hadn't been so lucky. We were shaken, but nobody got arrested.

Years later, at the same school, we were skating a newly built podium. This time, a cop approached us on foot, catching us off guard. Too close to run, we braced ourselves for the worst.

"Do you know those kids who just ran off?" he asked.

"No," we replied truthfully.

The officer sighed. "You know it's illegal to skate on school property, right?"

"Yes, officer."

What followed was a lecture—property damage, trespassing, all the usual talking points. We nodded along, hoping he'd leave it at that.

Instead, he pulled out his ticket book.

While writing us up, the officer glanced toward the fence-hoppers. "Those kids who ran—they'll get their day. But you kids? You're cooperating. I appreciate that. Once I'm done here, I'll be looking for them. If I catch them, they'll be charged with trespassing, defacing public property, and resisting arrest. You're lucky you stayed put."

He handed us our tickets, paused, and added, "I won't be back around for at least an hour. You kids get home safe."

We looked at each other, unsure whether to laugh or be annoyed. Was he giving us permission to keep skating?

The difference between these two run-ins was stark. In the first, we were faceless kids running from faceless cops. In the second, we were having a human-to-human interaction. The officer treated us like people—not criminals—and in return, we respected him.

It's a lot harder to disrespect someone when you're looking them in the eye. Skateboarding taught me that early on. When you're face-to-face with another human being, you have to confront your choices—you have to own them. And in a way, that's what skateboarding is all about: making choices, pushing boundaries, and owning the consequences—whether that means landing the trick or taking the ticket.

The More You Know

Kids today have become increasingly desensitized to confrontation, largely because of the internet. It has dramatically changed the way we navigate through life—literally. We don't need to remember how to get anywhere; Google takes care of that. Alexa can tell you when a package has arrived or remind you it's trash day. YouTube can catch you up on the Padres' most recent devastating loss or educate you on how to properly sharpen a chef's knife. With so much exposure, our emotional responsiveness to adverse situations diminishes. A kid who plays *World of Warcraft* for twenty hours a week might react differently to seeing a gun than a kid raised to understand and respect guns.

So, how does this relate to skateboarding? Well, I've had countless interactions with the police while skating. Over time, I've learned my rights and the importance of police in our society. Sure, I'd prefer cops focus on keeping the city safe from real dangers and give skateboarders a break. But run-ins with the law will always be part of street skating.

Some people fear the police because they've never had personal exposure or interaction with them. For some, this fear is justified. But when we encounter the unfamiliar or the misunderstood, fear is often the first response. Our instincts take over—fight, flight, or freeze. Whatever your body naturally does during an earthquake or tornado (shout out to the brave souls in Oklahoma), is probably how you'll respond to the unknown.

Skateboarding thrusts you into situations most upstanding citizens don't experience. Over the years, I've learned that treating the police with respect usually leads to better outcomes. When I didn't run but faced my consequences head-on, I saw in real time how honesty, attentiveness, and respect could change the dynamic.

Understanding the possible repercussions of your actions is a game changer. I know every time I street skate, I'm technically breaking the law. That's on me, not Karen. Sure, she's overreacting, but accepting responsibility for the irritation I've caused helps me keep a level head. Like skating itself, it's all about balance.

Skateboarding's outlaw nature is part of what makes it so unique! To get the most out of it, you have to respect the law—but that doesn't mean you shouldn't break it. The life lessons skateboarding instills far outweigh the fines and tickets you might collect along the way.

And just because something's illegal doesn't mean it's wrong. This country wouldn't have progressed as much as it has in the last hundred years without bold people willing to challenge unjust rules. I'm not saying skateboarders across the nation should rise up and demand universal legalization of skating in public spaces—but don't be afraid to push the boundaries when necessary.

Take Santa Monica's old, out-of-operation courthouse, for example. It's an iconic street spot known worldwide to skateboarders, but it was at risk of being bulldozed and sold to a private developer. A group of skaters, led by Eric Koston, worked with the city to purchase the courthouse with Nike's funding. As part of the agreement, the city mandated that no skateboarding could take place there until the deal was finalized—any violations would jeopardize the entire project.

One skateboarder from the group printed hundreds of flyers and plastered them on the courthouse ledges: *"Wait! Don't blow it. If you grind through this paper, you are blowing it for everyone."* For two months, not a single piece of paper had even a scratch.

When the deal was finalized, the complex was officially renamed the West LA Courthouse Skate Plaza.

Respect the law, but never stop jumping fences.

~

"Skateboarding is as much a mental sport as a physical one. You're constantly battling fear, doubt, and frustration." ~ **Stacy Peralta**

6

We're All In This Together

If you've gotten into skateboarding but none of your friends skate, don't worry. In skateboarding, making new friends comes naturally.

I started skateboarding later than most people—middle school instead of when I was four or five. My first skate buddies were classmates: Brandon, Matt, Torry, and Nick. None of us were particularly good; at the time, all we skated were curbs, and some of us were more into it than others. One day, after a solid curb sesh, Matt told me I was going to go pro one day and suggested I try getting sponsored by a local skate shop. I had no idea what that even meant. We'd only been skating for a few months—we had no business talking about getting sponsored. We were just little grommets pushing around, trying not to fall over our own feet. But the idea of one day getting free boards and gear? That sounded like the dream.

Fast forward to my sophomore year at Scripps Ranch High. My main skate crew was Dave, Boris, and Tyler. We'd usually head to Jerabeck Park after school to skate the three-stair. Other times, we'd book it to Horizon Skatepark in Bay Park. If Bryan wasn't with us, we'd always make plans to meet up on the weekend.

Bryan was the first of us to get sponsored—and it was well-deserved. The guy learned tricks so fast his brain could barely keep up. He got on with K-5, a shop in Poway that was the spot for any skater in the area. Shortly after, Bryan mentioned the shop was starting a team and had room for more riders. The news had Dave, Boris, Tyler, and me practically drooling. The idea of being on a shop team, getting free boards and shirts, was almost too much to process. It was every skater's first big milestone: getting sponsored. It meant someone saw potential in you, and now it was time to prove yourself.

Being sponsored by a shop like K-5 was a big deal. You were an ambassador for the store, representing it at local spots, contests, and in videos. K-5's deal was one free board and one shop shirt a month, plus discounts on additional gear. In exchange, you skated for them, wore their merch, and helped draw kids into the store. But shop teams had limited spots, and competition in the late '90s was fierce. Skateboarding was at its peak popularity—nearly every kid in Southern California either skated or had at least stood on a board in their friend's garage.

Realistically, there was no way all four of us would make the team. That didn't stop us from trying, though. We spent every weekend skating harder than ever, filming each other, and learning new tricks. The grind was relentless but rewarding. We pushed each other, hyped each other up, and celebrated every small victory. Bryan taught us that the key to progression wasn't just about talent; it was about showing up, putting in the work, and sticking with it no matter what.

That's the thing about skateboarding—it's a community. It doesn't matter where you come from, what you look like, or how good you are. If you're out there, pushing yourself and showing respect, you're part of the family. Some of my closest friendships were built through skateboarding. We supported each other, inspired each other, and shared in the triumphs and failures. No matter how competitive the scene got, it was always about the camaraderie.

We're all in this together.

Go Big or Go Home

Bryan told us to get our "sponsor me" tapes together for the K-5 team manager—a compilation of our best tricks, polished and ready to impress. Back then, editing wasn't exactly a smooth process. We started out using two VCRs: stop, play, record, repeat. It was clunky and time-consuming, but it got the job done. Then my parents bought me a Hi-8mm camera with a fisheye lens, and everything changed. Suddenly, we could record directly from the Hi-8 tape to a VHS tape. The picture quality was miles better.

Of course, this was long before smartphones with built-in wide-angle cameras and editing software made creating footage a breeze. Back then, if you wanted to show what you could do, you worked for it. But I digress.

When I finally turned in my tape to K-5, the shop was run by Tom and Jurgen Schultz—two awesome guys who handled everything personally. They were the heart of the shop, always giving their time to skaters in the community. I'll never forget the day they told me they liked my tape but wanted to see more.

"You've got potential," they said, "but we want to see how you progress. Bring us another tape—new tricks, new clips—when you're ready."

It wasn't the "yes" I'd hoped for, but I walked out of K-5 with a huge smile on my face. You might wonder why. I didn't get sponsored. I didn't achieve my goal. I had to start over and make a brand-new video—a process that could take months, maybe even a year. Shouldn't I have been crushed?

Here's the thing: it wasn't about the rejection. It was about the encouragement. K-5 didn't shut me down; they gave me hope. Maybe they told every kid the same thing, but it felt like they truly believed in me and my potential. That belief fueled me in a way nothing else could.

When we fail, we dig deeper. We try harder. That's exactly what I did with Dave, Boris, and Tyler. For months, we skated nonstop, feeding off each other's energy. There wasn't a drop of animosity between us. Instead, we pushed each other, which elevated us all. We were each other's biggest fans, each other's motivation. There's no room for negativity in skating. It's not about tearing someone else down. It's about building each other up and loving every second of the ride.

Getting Sponsored

Months passed, and I skated my ass off to put together my second "sponsor me" tape. This one was different. I had a few solid handrail tricks, ollied a huge gap, and threw in some technical flip tricks to grinds and slides. It was a big step up from my first tape, and I made sure it showed clear progression.

When it was ready, I walked into K-5 with the tape tucked under my left arm and my board in my right. I weaved through the surf clothing section, past the

Land on Both Feet

sunglasses display, and headed to the skate section where a few kids and their moms were waiting. Tom was there.

I hung back while he made his rounds, trying to keep my nerves in check. Finally, I handed him the tape. I'd never felt so excited and terrified at the same time. Tom was pumped to get it, though. He told me the team would watch it and let me know.

The waiting was brutal. Every time the phone rang, my heart jumped, only for it to be my mom telling me to come home for dinner. But eventually, *it happened*. Bryan called to tell me Tom and Jurgen wanted me to come into the shop. The way Bryan sounded on the phone gave me a good feeling.

Right after school, I booked it to Poway as fast as I could. Walking into the shop, I saw the smiles on everyone's faces—it was happening. Tom handed me my first K-5 board and congratulated me. I was beyond excited but tried to play it cool. That's always been my thing: act like you've been there before. But honestly, sometimes you just have to let the tiger out of the cage.

I remember setting up my first board with care, making sure everything was perfect. Cutting the grip tape in one smooth slice, pressing it down, tightening the bolts just right. I tested the trucks on the shop's carpet floor, rocking back and forth, getting a feel for it. The sense of accomplishment was overwhelming.

I casually broke the news to my parents that I got sponsored, even though it was a huge deal to me. They were proud, of course, though my dad would've been happier if I'd stuck with baseball. By that point, as a junior in high school, I could've probably walked onto the baseball team. But for me, that ship had sailed long ago.

My parents were always supportive, though. My mom even came to K-5 with me later to meet Tom and Jurgen and bought a few shirts to support the shop. K-5 quickly became my second home. It was where I hung out after school, watched skate videos, and talked shop with other skaters.

Not long after, Dave, Boris, and Tyler all got sponsored by K-5 too. We weren't just friends anymore—we were a team. Looking back, it's crazy to think that out of thousands of skaters in North County, five of the six spots on the K-5 team went to my closest friends.

The sixth guy was Dustin Begovich, who went to Poway High. He became a great friend, especially since he was just as into filming and editing as I was. By then, we had computers—not really for "school," despite what we told our parents, but for editing and storing our skate clips.

K-5 held an annual demo in the shop's parking lot. They'd block off the area, set up ramps and obstacles, and let the team skate while the neighborhood came to watch. Hundreds of kids showed up. DJs played music, food carts sold tacos and burgers—it was a huge half-day event. Sometimes we'd have best trick contests, going head-to-head against each other. To the younger kids in the crowd, we were like celebrities. It was an incredible feeling.

But this wasn't the final destination—it was just the beginning. With recognition came responsibilities. And we were ready to rise to the occasion.

CASL

Once the team was set, Tom and Jurgen called us in for a mandatory meeting along with their second new shops team, to lay out their expectations. This is when we met the north county guys like Mason, Mike, Travis and Dylan. If you are in the skate community you'll know the name Dylan Rieder. (R.I.P Dylan and Travis)

Tom and Jurgen wanted us to keep pushing ourselves—progressing, filming in the streets, and shooting high-quality photos. If we were lucky enough to land a photo in a magazine with the K-5 logo visible on our boards or shirts, they'd reward us with a crisp hundred dollar bill. That was a lot of money back then. That incentive alone was enough to get us hyped, but they weren't done yet.

They also wanted us to compete in the California Amateur Skateboard League, better known as CASL. CASL was a proving ground for young shop-sponsored skaters, hosting a series of competitions throughout the year. Each skater competed in their respective age group, and back in my day, we had two sixty-second runs in the prelims. If your scores were high enough, you'd move on to the finals, where you'd get another two sixty-second runs. The top scores from the finals decided the winners.

There was more to it than individual glory, though. Shops could also compete for the title of "best all-around team." I don't remember the exact points system, but it motivated us not to give up, even if we had a bad day. Sure, we all wanted to perform our best individually, but winning as part of your team was just as rewarding. All for one, and one for all.

Tom and Jurgen made it clear: the goal was to win the best shop award, and to ride for K-5, we had to commit to every CASL competition each month. These contests were spread across Southern California, from San Diego to Ventura. It was a grind, but we were all in.

The competitions were no joke. CASL was a breeding ground for future pros, and skating alongside names like Paul Rodriguez and Torey Pudwill was both inspiring and intimidating. Still, I was proud to rep the K-5 team. We weren't just a group of kids who skated together—we were a unit. We looked out for each other, pushed each other, and celebrated each other's successes.

After skating in CASL competitions for a while, you started recognizing the same faces from other cities. Naturally, rivals emerged. Some kids were better than others, creating an unspoken hierarchy. Everyone fell somewhere on the spectrum. I never won a contest outright—second place was my best finish—but consistently placing in the top five felt good.

Skateboarding contests are a strange beast. On one hand, you want to win, and in the back of your mind, you wouldn't mind if someone else had an off day. But openly rooting against someone? That's not skateboarding. Sure, there were a few pricks in the scene, but most skaters genuinely want to see others land their tricks. Contests feel more like giant sessions, where the energy and support from everyone around you elevate your skating. The best sessions—and the best contests—happen when everyone is pushing each other to the limit.

If you've watched Street League or Olympic skateboarding, you've probably noticed this dynamic. The skaters competing against each other are often close friends, cheering each other on and genuinely admiring each other's performances. Sure, some skaters excel at contests —Nyjah Houston, for example, is one of the best. I'd go so far as to say he's the Michael Jordan of contest skating. He's not *just* a contest skater, either; his street parts are next-level. But in contests, when the pressure is on, Nyjah is clutch. That said, he doesn't always win. There's a handful of pros who constantly give him a run for his money.

Take Yuto Horigome, for example. He absolutely

shredded at the Olympics, taking home gold in both 2020 and 2024. Watching him skate was incredible, and while Nyjah was visibly upset at his own performance, that didn't stop him from congratulating Yuto. That's skateboarding. It's about respect, support, and community—even in the heat of competition.

Mainstream vs. Subculture

Between 2010 and 2015, skateboarding underwent a massive shift toward commercialization. Skaters like Nyjah Houston started making millions from sponsors, with big names like Target and Audi entering the scene. But long before mainstream brands took notice, skateboarding thrived as a subculture. It didn't need mainstream media, corporate backing, or the spotlight of Street League to survive. Skateboarding isn't like other sports—it's rooted in individuality, community, and rebellion.

Rob Dyrdek's creation of Street League, now essentially the Major League of Skateboarding, played a key role in skateboarding's commercialization. Rob wasn't just a business mogul; he was a respected skater in his own right, riding for Alien Workshop and DC Shoes during my childhood. Coming from inside the community gave him credibility and allowed him to build a league that skaters respected.

While mainstream exposure has brought new profits and opportunities, it's also been a two-way street. The public gets to see big contests and jaw-dropping tricks, while skaters competing on that stage benefit from international recognition. As long as the relationship stays balanced, it's a win for everyone.

That said, the essence of skateboarding isn't found

under the bright lights of televised contests. It lives in the streets, in battles fought on schoolyards and in drainage ditches. It thrives in creativity and community—in the way skaters transform everyday architecture into art. The public sees the polished performances at Street League, but they'll never fully grasp the raw, unfiltered energy of a late-night session on a Hubba ledge or a secret spot only skaters know about.

Skateboarding has always been about more than tricks or trophies. It's about pushing boundaries—on your board, in your creativity, and within your community. The mainstream can have its contests and corporate sponsors, but the soul of skateboarding will always belong to those who keep it alive where it matters most: in the streets.

The Next Generation

Kids these days have access to opportunities we could only dream of growing up. The skateparks built in the last decade have completely transformed the landscape. Many parks now emulate street plazas, with obstacles like ledges, stairs, and handrails designed to replicate real-world street skating spots. Skateboarders like Tony Hawk, Rob Dyrdek and Kanten Russell played a massive role in this transformation, stepping in to design parks themselves rather than leaving it to people who didn't understand the sport. This shift moved skateparks away from the old-school ramps and half-pipes and turned them into training grounds that help advance street skating in a safe and legal environment.

Traditional parks with transitions still exist, of course, but now kids can practice flipping into handrails or grinding A-frame ledges every day—without the fear of getting chased off by security guards. It's no wonder skateboarding has progressed so rapidly. The tricks kids are pulling off today—flipping in and out of grinds, cruising hundred-foot kink rails—were unthinkable just a decade ago.

Skateboarding's accessibility has always been one of its greatest strengths. You don't need a team, a coach, or a schedule. All you need is your board and a slab of cement. The rise of skate plazas has only made it easier to hone your skills. And then there's YouTube.

YouTube has revolutionized skateboarding in ways no one could've imagined. When I was growing up, skate media was hard to come by. Videos were sold at skate shops (if you even had one nearby), and they only came out occasionally. By the time you saw a trick in a video, it could've been years since it was landed. Keeping up with trends or the cutting edge of skating was nearly impossible for the average skater.

Today, it's a whole new world. With a click of a button, skaters can see what's possible on YouTube, Instagram, Facebook, or X. Tricks can be watched, analyzed in slow motion, rewound, and replayed. Tutorials, spot breakdowns, and endless footage are just a few clicks away. This limitless access to inspiration and information has driven skateboarding to unimaginable heights.

But what makes skateboarding truly special isn't just the progression or the accessibility. It's the inclusivity. Skateboarding doesn't care who you are. We aren't girls or boys, parents or kids, teachers or students, baristas or customers, cops or rappers. We're skateboarders. You don't need to be seven feet tall or have started training at three. You don't need to look, act, or be a certain way. Skateboarding is for everyone, everywhere.

In a world that often feels divided, skateboarding is a

reminder of what unity looks like. Too much hate fills our streets, too much rage fills our roads. People fear what they don't know. If you don't see the world as I do, then you must be against me. This mindset divides societies, pinning people against one another. But skateboarding has taught me to see past those walls.

No matter who you are or where you come from, everyone has something to contribute. We all have a responsibility to help each other grow. Our community is only as strong as our weakest links. Skateboarding gives us the chance to learn from one another—not just tricks, but life experiences, perspectives, and values.

The person skating down the sidewalk isn't just someone who shares your hobby. They share your love for this art. They share your belief in its power and beauty. They understand what it feels like to land a trick after hours of trying, to roll away from failure, and to push through life one kick at a time. In skateboarding, there's no prejudice, no preconceived notions—unless they're pushing Mongo, of course.

We are skateboarders, and we're all pushing through life together.

"Every slam is just another step closer to landing the trick. It's about how many times you're willing to get up." ~ **Eric Koston**

7

Battles Are Uphill, and the Peaks Are Made of Marble

Skateboarding is a constant tug-of-war between highs and lows. Some days, you're unstoppable. Your flick is perfect, your balance steady, your timing precise. Everything just clicks. You cruise through the park landing tricks that usually give you trouble, making it look effortless—like you were born to skate. Those are the golden days, the ones that remind you why you started in the first place. They're the days to pull out the camera and finally film that trick you've been dreaming about.

But then there are *those* days. The ones where nothing works. Tricks you've landed a hundred times suddenly feel impossible. Every attempt ends with frustration. You get wheelbite on a lone pebble, sending you tumbling. A stray water bottle rolls into your line, and you barely avoid slamming. Doubt creeps in. You start questioning your stance, your movements, the techniques you've trusted for years. When that happens, you might as well pack it in for the day —because skateboarding isn't just physical. It's mental.

People who play golf understand this. I've been golfing

since before I can remember—literally. My parents have footage of me swinging a golf club at a driving range when I was three or four. I don't even remember it. I played for my high school team, too, at Torrey Pines South, one of the most challenging courses in the world. My best score there was 79; my worst was well into the hundreds. How can you be so good one day and utterly terrible the next? Golf, like skateboarding, is a sport of precision. A small misstep—a shift in balance, a slight change in timing—and everything falls apart.

But skateboarding is more demanding. It's the most humbling activity I've ever done. It has the power to obliterate your confidence, leave you physically wrecked, and force you to rebuild from scratch. It's relentless.

Take manuals, for example. Widely regarded as one of the most technical tricks, they require an insane amount of concentration and balance. You're riding on just two wheels —your back ones for a manual, your front ones for a nose manual—usually across a manual pad with a curb up and a curb down. For beginners, simply riding normally is hard enough; balancing on two wheels takes years of practice. Landing flip-in, flip-out manuals consistently demands near-superhuman focus.

The more you try a trick, the harder it becomes to stay mentally sharp. Once frustration sets in, you're in trouble. It's a slippery slope. Every failed attempt feels heavier than the last, and suddenly, you're doubting everything. You tell yourself you're close—and maybe you are—but the mental strain of repeated failure can crush you. Very rarely have I landed a trick right after losing my cool.

Meltdowns happen. Some skaters channel frustration into confidence, using it to hype themselves up for risky tricks. They scream, toss their boards, and build momentum for their next attempt. That's not me. When I've melted down, it's been out of anger at myself—doubting my abilities, tossing my board like a toddler mid-tantrum. And I hate it. Skateboarding is supposed to be fun, but sometimes it makes you want to smash everything in sight.

At that point, there's no use continuing. Pushing through frustration rarely works. The best move is to stop and reset—whether that means taking a break or coming back the next day. But most skaters don't quit. It's not in our DNA. We keep going, even when we're physically and mentally drained, convinced that the next attempt will be the one. And sometimes, it is. But other times, it's not.

I've been there more times than I can count. The worst feeling is knowing you're capable of landing a trick but still walking away empty-handed. For me, it was the kickflip nose manual nollie flip out. I'd landed kickflip nose manuals. I'd landed nose manual nollie flips. But putting them together? That was my white whale.

I must've tried that trick over a thousand times across four separate sessions. I never rolled away. I went home each time, laid in bed, and replayed every failed attempt in my head, wondering what could've been. It eats at you. You know that failure is part of the game—it's a lesson you learn early as a skater. You fail until you succeed. But when you've tried a trick thousands of times without luck, you start to wonder: *How do you actually overcome it?*

∿

When to Retreat

IF YOU'VE TRIED A TRICK THOUSANDS OF TIMES AND STILL HAVEN'T landed it, here's the hard truth: you don't yet have the skills to pull it off. Plain and simple—and yeah, harsh. But it's the reality. It's a reality I wish I'd recognized sooner in several instances. So, what do you do about it? You break it down.

In my case, I wasn't consistent enough with either part of the trick. My head was in the clouds. I could land a kickflip nose manual maybe one out of twenty tries. Same for a nose manual nollie flip—one out of twenty.

Now, mathematically, that means I should have been able to land a kickflip nose manual nollie flip once every 400 tries. By that logic, having tried the trick a few thousand times, I *should* have landed it. But skateboarding doesn't work like math class. When you stop for the day or take a break, your odds reset. And after two hours of trying a trick, frustration and exhaustion set in, crushing your chances even more.

If you average one attempt per minute, you're getting about 120 tries in two hours—if you're not taking breaks, trips to the water fountain, or inhaling a bag of Salsa Verde Doritos. And let's be honest, the last few dozen tries? You're so mentally and physically drained that your attempts get slower, more hesitant, and less effective.

Looking at it from that perspective, the odds of landing that trick faster than expected were slim. It's clear now that I needed to improve on the individual components of the trick first. Instead of trying to brute-force my way to one lucky landing, I should have focused on consistency— landing each part of the trick one out of ten tries instead of one out of twenty. It seems obvious now, but back then, it never crossed my mind.

The only real path to landing that trick was to practice the two parts separately until they became second nature.

But instead, I stubbornly kept trying the full trick over and over, convinced that I could will it into existence.

Accepting that you need more practice and preparation to do something you *think* you can do isn't easy. I made excuse after excuse for why I didn't land the trick on any given day. *My balance was off yesterday. I just got new shoes and hadn't broken them in.* But the truth was simpler: I wasn't prepared. I spent too much time trying to film tricks I couldn't land consistently, instead of honing the skills I needed to get better.

Focusing solely on landing a trick—without putting in the work to train for it—limits your ability to grow. Your odds don't magically improve just because you've tried it 700 times. Progress comes from deliberate practice, not sheer repetition.

If professional athletes only performed during games, they wouldn't last long. They train between matches, almost every day, breaking down their mechanics, studying their techniques, and building their skills. Skateboarding is no different. Training is essential. But it's easy to overlook, especially when the thrill of "just going for it" clouds your judgment.

If I'd spent just one week practicing kickflip nose manuals alone, I probably would've improved enough to give myself a real shot at landing the trick. But back then, the difference between "going for it" and "practicing" wasn't clear to me. I was too caught up in the excitement of trying to pull off the impossible.

The lesson? Sometimes you have to step back, assess your weaknesses, and train the skills you're missing. Skateboarding isn't just about the big moments when everything comes together—it's about the work you put in when no one's watching.

When to Keep Pushing

Battles are uphill—literally, sometimes. You have to dig deep, give it everything you've got, and, against all odds, trust yourself to come out on top.

Some of my most memorable battles were quite literally uphill. I was living in San Francisco at the time, and there was this massive cement launch ramp tucked away in the back of a shipping container yard. It was almost head-high, steep, and intimidating. Most skaters didn't bother trying flip tricks off it because of how much speed you'd need just to make it up with enough momentum. But the skate gods had blessed this spot with a glorious detail: metal coping running all the way up to the top.

It was an epic spot—if you could deal with the cracked runway and the stray rocks scattered everywhere. A push broom was practically mandatory before each session. For me, the up-ledge was backside, which wasn't my strong suit. I wasn't naturally a ledge skater, though I'd tried. When I was just starting out, I built a box in my backyard using wooden crates, a piece of plywood, and coping from an old bed frame my parents were tossing. (Look at me, locally foraging materials—what a model citizen.)

But here's the catch: the coping on my homemade ledge was only six feet long, while the two crates together measured eight. I had to decide which side it would end on, so I went with frontside. That choice forever shaped my bag of tricks on ledges. To this day, I can still frontside nose-blunt a ledge, but a backside 5-0? That scares the shit out of me.

Enter this up-ledge. My initial idea was a crook 180, but Bryan went and ruined that plan by pulling off a crooked grind all the way up to the top and popping out. It was insane. My crook 180 would've looked pathetic in comparison. So, I set my sights on a backside 5-0 180—a trick I was absolutely terrible at.

About ten minutes in, disaster struck. I missed the ledge, and since it sloped upward, I didn't fall down—I fell *into* it. Full speed. Zero time to brace. It was straight to the sack.

After hobbling around, screaming, crying, and laughing in equal parts, I pulled myself together. Logic told me to stop. But something deeper told me to keep going. Call it intuition, gut instinct, or pure stupidity—sometimes you just have to listen to that voice, even when your body and mind are screaming otherwise.

I brushed off my oversized jeans, took a few hesitant attempts to get the feel for it again, and psyched myself up for one last try. *Just go for it.* I threw my board down, pushed hard, and gave it everything I had. I popped at the perfect moment, balanced cleanly through the grind, and scooped the 180 out with a bit of swag. Rolling away, I felt like the king of back 5-0 180s.

That should've been the end of it. But, drunk on success, I convinced myself to come back a few weeks later and try a backside tailslide—a trick I was even worse at.

You can probably guess what happened next.

Yup. I sacked the ledge. Again. Twice. For the record, nobody sacks ledges, and I did it twice on the same one.

After the pain subsided and I regained movement in my leg, the same voice popped into my head: *Try again.* I swore it off, told myself it wasn't worth it, but the thought wouldn't leave. Eventually, I caved. Jesse and Ryan were there that day, and even they were surprised I kept going. Hours later, I managed to land a backside tail fakie. I didn't slide as far as I wanted, but it was enough for me to rationalize never trying it again.

Not every battle ends in triumph. Some are speed bumps, while others are mountains with peaks you'll never see. The key is listening to that voice inside you. Sometimes it feels like it's steering you straight into failure, but you'll never know until you push through and see where it takes you.

True Dedication

As humans, we all dream big. For me, it started with baseball—I wanted to become a professional player. But skateboarding changed everything. The life of a professional skateboarder became *the* dream: your name on the bottom of a board, traveling the world, doing what you love with your friends, all on your own schedule. It was freedom, creativity, and passion wrapped into one.

As we've discussed, fulfilling any dream requires setting clear goals. In skateboarding, the path to going pro typically looks like this:

1. You learn to skate and dedicate yourself to improving every day.
2. You start filming your tricks and get sponsored by a local shop.
3. You enter local contests, get your name out there in the community, and keep progressing.
4. You earn "flow" sponsorships from a board or shoe company through your shop sponsor.
5. You work relentlessly, eventually earning an amateur spot on a team.

6. Finally, with enough dedication and skill, you hope to turn pro.

That's the roadmap. No shortcuts, no get-rich-quick schemes, no inheritance to give you a head start. Everyone starts from zero, and every step forward requires relentless effort. In skateboarding, we call those steps *battles*.

Skateboarding teaches you to embrace this reality quickly. Progress comes slowly, day by day. Each small improvement builds on the last, intentionally moving you closer to your goal. It's not about luck or magic; it's about consistent, deliberate effort.

Sometimes, though, you hit a battle that feels impossible to win. In those moments, it's easy to feel defeated. You want to overcome the obstacle, but the larger goal looms so far in the distance that it feels hopeless. The temptation to skip ahead, to concede this particular fight, is strong—but doing so can come back to bite you, like an unforgiving up-ledge.

Here's the thing: those seemingly impossible battles *are* the path to your larger goal. Progress doesn't come from avoiding challenges; it comes from tackling them head-on, even when the odds seem stacked against you.

I've learned this the hard way, and over time, I've developed a cycle to live by. When working toward a distant goal, the journey can feel overwhelming. Obsessing over the ultimate destination can actually stop you from reaching it (more on that in Chapter 10). Instead of fixating on dreams, resolutions, or viral TikTok challenges, I've learned to set *standards*.

Standards are different from goals. Goals are the destination; standards are the expectations you set for yourself along the way. They're the habits, routines, and values that guide your daily actions, keeping you grounded and moving forward. Reaching a goal can feel impossible, but living up to your standards—day in and day out—that's entirely within your control, right here and now.

True dedication isn't about chasing a dream endlessly or waiting for a lucky break. It's about showing up every day, holding yourself to your standards, and trusting that those small, intentional steps will lead you where you need to go.

The Cycle

It's easy to fall into the trap of constantly looking toward tomorrow, forgetting to celebrate what you've accomplished today. Skateboarding teaches you the importance of recognizing and rewarding yourself along the journey—it's what makes the process worth it. It's not about winning the war; it's about savoring the victories in each individual battle.

I've never bought a million-dollar house, nor did I turn pro, but skateboarding has given me a perspective on the cycle of ambition. Let's imagine, for a moment, what it would feel like to finally achieve that ultimate dream.

You're determined to buy a million-dollar dream home. You live below your means, make smart financial decisions, and work tirelessly to save enough. Maybe it takes ten years, but eventually, you make it happen. You've done it! You've qualified for the life you dreamed of years ago.

But here's the twist: by the time you get there, a million-dollar home no longer feels like the dream. Inflation, changing markets, and shifting tastes mean that what you wanted back then now costs three million dollars. Plus, technology has advanced, and your vision has evolved. Now you want a smart home, upgraded security, and a completely different design.

Suddenly, you're back at square one, committing another decade to chasing the *new* dream. And what happens when you finally catch up? Maybe at sixty, you walk into your backyard, sit by your infinity pool with a cold beer, and think, *This is the life.* And for a while, it is.

But life doesn't stop. Monday comes, and you're still running the company that paid for the house because those payments don't make themselves. You didn't win the lottery. You worked hard and accomplished your dream, but at what cost? You might wonder where all the time went, asking yourself the ultimate question: *When do we stop chasing a better life and start living in the one we have?*

Skateboarding, thankfully, bakes these moments into the journey. It gives you opportunities to pause, to appreciate the progress you've made, and to feel the joy of where you are right now.

Take a marble surface, for example. Across the skateboarding world, marble is the holy grail. Grinding a marble ledge is pure perfection. You could do it over and over, and every time it feels just as pristine as the last. Riding on marble is like taking a Sunday drive through the countryside in a convertible, a reprieve from life's grind. It's not just a trick—it's an experience. Satisfaction, accomplishment, recognition, and joy all wrapped into one.

And it's not just the marble ledge. It's landing a trick you dreamed of the night before. It's a session with old friends and new ones, pushing each other to be better. It's getting a trick on film you thought was impossible.

These moments document our progression, offering validation and recognition along the way. You landed that trick you've been chasing, and now you can rewatch it forever.

The cycle of ambition doesn't have to be an endless chase for something far off. Skateboarding teaches us to find fulfillment in the here and now, in the small victories that make up the larger journey. The question isn't just how far we can go but how much we can appreciate along the way.

You train. These are the early morning workouts, the late-night sessions, the countless hours of preparation. This is when you set the standard, conditioning your mind and body for the battles ahead.

You fight. You push yourself, and often, failure comes first. That's expected—it's part of the process. You accept failure as an integral step toward progress. You go home, replay it in your mind, and reflect.

Then you train again. You put in the work needed to overcome that failure. You prepare, adjusting your approach, sharpening your skills. You return to the fight, and this time, you succeed.

But then, you stop. You take a moment to recognize the progress you've made. You enjoy the victory, bask in the accomplishment, and reward yourself for the effort it took to get there.

Once the high fades, you reflect. You relive what it took to reach this point—the sweat, the setbacks, the moments of doubt you pushed through. In that reflection, you realize how far you've come. You see that the work has paid off, and with it, you've raised the bar. You're not who you were when you started; you're better, stronger, and ready for the next battle.

And so, you repeat.

This cycle becomes your standard. Over time, as you grow older and wiser, it begins to weave itself into your everyday life. You learn to create milestones where there were none, moments to celebrate progress, no matter how small. You keep moving forward, but not without appreciating what you've accomplished along the way.

The cycle becomes easier to navigate. You start to anticipate how much time, preparation, and effort a goal will require. You waste less energy, succeed more often, and recover faster. Bumps along the road don't throw you off course—they're already accounted for in the system. You keep moving forward.

In the end, it's the battles we'll look back on. Some will be easy, mere steps along the way. Others will be hard-fought and unforgettable. But after every battle won, you face a choice:

One path leads to a pristine marble surface, where you can glide in absolute bliss, savoring the perfection of the moment. The other path winds up a mountain, steep and challenging, leading you closer to glory.

It's up to you to decide when to keep your eyes ahead and when to pause and skate the marble.

"Skateboarding is the epitome of freedom. It's not about winning—it's about self-expression." ~ **Christian Hosoi**

8

Skill Isn't Measured by What You Can Do, but How You Do What You Can

There are things in life we're all drawn to. Some are easy to explain—like tacos. They're delicious, simple, and endlessly versatile. (And yes, tacos *are* their own food group. Don't let anyone tell you otherwise.) Breakfast tacos with chorizo and eggs, street tacos, fish tacos, BBQ tacos, even dessert tacos—the possibilities are infinite.

Other things we're drawn to are harder to explain. A photograph, a bridge, a song. Out of the millions that exist in the world, why do those specific ones resonate?

For me, skateboarding was one of those things. Early in my journey, my dream was crystal clear: I wanted to turn pro. The idea of skating every day with my friends, traveling the world, and making a living doing what I loved sounded like pure freedom. Who wouldn't want that?

After getting sponsored by K-5, I was laser-focused on making that dream a reality. I didn't have a clear roadmap, but I knew one thing: I needed to improve. Whenever I watched professional skaters' videos, I'd compare their tricks to my own sponsor tape. The difference in skill was glaring—they were just better. But that was okay. I'd eventually learn one of the most important lessons of my journey:

You can't compare the beginning of your journey to the middle of someone else's.

It's the quickest way to sabotage your success.

Still, one thing stood out when I compared their videos to mine: my bag of tricks was tiny. If I wanted to go pro, I needed more tricks—and harder ones at that.

So that became my goal. I threw myself into practice, determined to expand my trick catalog. I needed to learn more flip tricks, master more ledge tricks, and take what I already knew to the next level. That meant moving basic grind and slide tricks to handrails—bigger, more intimidating, and where small miscalculations come at a cost.

But here's the thing: my desperation to turn pro caused me to make a few crucial missteps along the way. My focus was scattered, my approach sometimes misguided. I was so fixated on the dream that I didn't always stop to think about *how* I was getting there. Let's break it down: what I did, why I did it, and, maybe, what I should have done instead to better achieve my goal.

Blinded by the Light

At the same skate camp where I met Bryan, I met another kid named Cheyne Magnusson. Cheyne was crazy cool—full of energy and awesome to skate with. He had serious street skills and was solid at vert skating too (the massive half-pipes Tony Hawk is famous for). Cheyne was the one who convinced me to drop in on a vert ramp for the first time.

Through Cheyne, I eventually met his dad, Tony Magnusson—a professional vert skater in the '80s and '90s. Tony had invented a few iconic tricks, including the first kickflip frontside air. Missile Park had a vert ramp, and Cheyne, Bryan, and I would attempt to skate it while Tony casually threw down 540s like it was nothing. And he was almost forty at the time—the same age I am now. Life moves fast.

Tony was also the founder of Osiris Shoes, a massive name in the late '90s. Even if you've never touched a skateboard, you probably remember the D3s, Dave Mayhew's pro shoe. They transcended skate culture, becoming a pop phenomenon.

When I turned fifteen, Tony gave me a summer job at the Osiris warehouse. I was stoked—working for a skate company was a dream come true. My first task? Put stickers on every single Peter Smolik shoe box to correct a misprinted credit. Thousands of boxes. For two weeks, eight hours a day, all I did was sticker boxes. It was the longest, most monotonous, yet most exciting two weeks of my life.

After that, they let me stay for the summer, learning the ropes: packing orders, taking inventory, fulfilling shipments. I was surrounded by pros and industry veterans, soaking in every moment. Arcade Skateboards shared the warehouse, which was how I met Jason Rogers, another iconic pro. Jason became a mentor of sorts, guiding me through skateboarding and life.

As I got to know Jason, I helped Bryan get sponsored by Arcade. Once that happened, we started skating together regularly. Most of the Arcade team was based in L.A., but our San Diego missions were just a few of us—Jason, Bryan, Casey Rigney, and me. These guys were on a different level, but they always included me, encouraged me, and pushed me to improve.

Back then, getting a trick on video was only part of the game. You also needed photos for magazines like *Transworld* or *Thrasher*. A photo credit in a magazine was everything—it introduced you to the skate world. When we didn't have a photographer, Jason taught me how to use a film camera while he shot video. I even had a couple of photos published in *Transworld*. Seeing my name in print— or even Jason's name on a photo I took—was surreal.

Skating with these guys, I felt like I was on the right path. At K-5, Tom and Jurgen let us create a team video called *All I Do Is Skate*. Dustin and I filmed and edited it ourselves. It took a year to finish, and when it hit the shelves at K-5 shops, it was incredible to see something we made being sold. That video gave each of us a new part to showcase for sponsors.

Eventually, I was introduced to Jeff, who was opening a skate shop in Poway called Urban Board Shop. He was looking to start a team and thought I'd be a good fit. I parted ways with K-5 on good terms and became Urban's first rider. Jeff promised he could help me get on flow with a few companies, and soon, I was being flowed shoes by Savier, clothes by Billabong, and sunglasses by Oakley.

By this time, I was progressing. I could flip into grinds, skate ten-stair rails, and hold my own in local contests. But with more sponsorships came more pressure. I felt like I had to constantly prove myself—not just to my sponsors but to myself. So, I skated nonstop, trying to land bigger tricks and create better footage.

For two years, I tried to balance skating and college at San Diego State University. Between classes, partying, and filming, I barely kept up with school. My English professor, Glenn, gave me my only A—not because I earned it, but because he liked me. I began to realize I couldn't keep living in two worlds.

I thought I was doing all the right things. I surrounded myself with better skaters who pushed me. I filmed nonstop, had sponsors, and was part of a team.I told myself that if I could create a video part on par with the pros, my sponsors would have no choice but to put me on the official team. But no matter how hard I worked, I wasn't progressing fast enough.

IF ONLY I'D LISTENED

Nearly twenty years later, looking back on the trajectory, I find myself asking: *What happened? Where did it go wrong?*

At first, my eyes were on the prize—glued to it, in fact. I was consumed by the dream. My best friend turned pro, and all the skaters I worked with were pros. I even tagged along on one of Arcade's cross-country demo road trips, riding in the RV with the team. At a few shop demos, I was allowed to skate alongside them, even though I wasn't officially on the team. It was intoxicating—and suffocating. My desire to be in their shoes choked out everything else.

I was obsessed with improving. I had the motivation, sure, but I approached it the wrong way. Instead of embracing the natural progression—building skills one step at a time—I tried to cut corners. In my mind, the best way to prove I was good enough was to film the hardest tricks the pros were landing. The ones in the middle? I skipped those entirely. Filming became my sole focus, to the point where I stopped skating for fun. I was constantly on my board but rarely practicing in a way that actually improved my abilities.

By the time I was a sophomore in college, I was pretty good. I still went on skate missions with Bryan and Jason before they moved to LA. Arcade was thriving, and Jason had just launched a new wheel company, Autobahn, which instantly became *the* place to ride. Even Mark Appleyard was on Autobahn. I thought I was good enough to at least get flow from either Autobahn or Arcade, but Jason always saw me as the warehouse kid—the little brother of the company.

It bugged me for a long time. I never said anything to Jason, but I'm sure he knew.

One day, I met up with Bryan, Casey, and Jason at the warehouse. Bryan and I brought a mini picnic table to skate in the alley. As we warmed up, Bryan put on a clinic—half-cab crook, backside tail, frontside crook. Then, just for fun, he nearly nailed a half-cab crook revert on his first try. Jason had just bought a new digital camera—one of the first of its kind. Yep, I was on Earth before digital cameras existed. He started snapping photos.

I was working on a crooked grind 180. Casey was nollie nosegrinding the same table. After the session, we all looked at the pictures Jason had taken. The best shot of the day? Me, mid-trick.

The photo was amazing, but it didn't sit right with me. I hadn't even landed the trick. I felt deflated. A crook 180 wasn't anywhere near the difficulty level of what Bryan or Casey were doing, and yet they didn't care about filming their tricks—they just landed them, laughed, and moved on. I, on the other hand, was obsessed with getting every-thing on video, even if it wasn't perfect.

That day, Jason pulled me aside and said, "Don't worry so much about filming. Just skate to have fun and practice. The tricks will come." It was solid advice—probably the best I'd ever gotten—but it fell on deaf ears.

In my mind, there was no time. I was already in college, and teenagers like Paul Rodriguez, who I competed against in CASL, were turning pro. I thought if I could just film enough great tricks fast enough, someone—maybe Jason—would notice. But that's not how it works. You don't shortcut your way to success. You have to put in the work, brick by brick.

At the time, I thought I *was* putting in the work. I was mimicking the pros, wasn't I? But I didn't understand the difference between practice and performance. I skipped the foundation entirely. Ironically, it wasn't until I moved to San Francisco and let go of the dream of "making it" that I truly started to improve.

MY FAVORITE SKATER

I moved up to San Francisco my junior year and majored in cinema. I met new friends, new skaters, and my first real girlfriend, Amanda, and started building a life in the Bay. I held on to a few sponsors and still skated almost every weekend, but over time, I let them fizzle out as my vision for the next five to ten years began to shift.

San Francisco is a skateboard Mecca. The city's architecture and layout create endless street spots: Pier 7, Embarcadero, Third and Army. These world-famous locations were spots I'd only dreamed of skating, and now they were in my backyard. For the first time in years, I was skating purely for fun—and almost immediately, everything changed. Without the pressure to prove myself to sponsors, I rediscovered my love for skateboarding. As that love returned, so did my confidence, and with it, my ability improved.

My intentions shifted. Instead of chasing the hardest tricks I couldn't land, I started working on perfecting the ones I could. I still filmed, but not obsessively. I'd practice a trick until it felt natural before ever considering filming it. The result? Filming became less of an overwhelming battle and more of a rewarding challenge. My passion for skating was completely renewed.

During my San Francisco days, my favorite skater was Stephan Janoski. I was lucky enough to be flowed shoes from Savier still at the time, the company he rode for. I even took a trip to Portland to skate their warehouse and film with their team manager.

Stephan was one of the top pros at Savier, but he didn't have an endless bag of tricks like some others. What set him apart was his style—effortless, smooth, magnetic. Watching him skate wasn't just impressive; it was inspiring. Even his basic tricks felt like art in motion. Whenever I watched his videos, I couldn't wait to grab my board and hit the streets.

Around this time, Bryan had stepped out of the spotlight and moved to Lake Tahoe. He'd been a household name for a while, but when Arcade folded, he couldn't find another board company to offer him a pro deal. Meanwhile, I was finishing college. One weekend, Bryan called me up about skating in Sacramento with a friend of his—and Stephan Janoski.

Um, yes, please.

Growing up, I was surrounded by pros all the time. But this was different. Stephan was one of my all-time favorite skaters. I couldn't have been more excited, but I knew I had to play it cool.

We met at Stephan's house before heading to a few spots. He wasn't in the mood to film, so we just cruised around a schoolyard, skating flat ground. Watching him casually throw down nollie half-cab flips was surreal. He wasn't trying to impress anyone, but his style, his swagger —whatever you want to call it—was undeniable. It was something I'd always admired but hadn't yet realized I wanted to emulate.

That day taught me something important. Progress doesn't come from mimicking someone else's path. We all get lost in chasing goals, thinking there's a "clear" way to achieve them. But the truth is, every journey is different. Just because one road led someone else to success doesn't mean it's the right one for you.

Looking back, I wish I'd understood that sooner. Instead of obsessing over filming, I should've dedicated myself to building a solid foundation. I should've taken a year off from filming, skating four to five days a week, focusing on the basics: kickflips, tailslides, grinds—over and over again. I should've pushed myself until landing those tricks felt automatic. That's the foundation, and it kills me now that I didn't take the time to perfect it.

The best skaters—Nyjah Houston, for example—practice the basics every single day. Watch his *Send Saturdays* series on YouTube. When he skates a handrail, he warms up by rifling off basic tricks. Sure, he can land incredibly technical tricks, but he starts with the fundamentals to keep them sharp.

I, on the other hand, took the opposite approach. I'd warm up with a boardslide or grind, then jump straight to the trick I wanted to film. It made sense at the time—I wanted to maximize my chances of landing the trick before the session ended. But in the long run, that approach didn't help me grow. When you spend all your time chasing only the hardest tricks, you lose the consistency you had with the simpler ones.

Skateboarding, like anything, requires repetition. Mastery isn't about chasing the big moment—it's about building the skills that make those moments possible.

BACK TO THE BASICS

When I was a kid, going to Padres spring training was the highlight of my year. My dad took us every season with his best friend, Big Mike, and Big Mike's son, Little Mike. It was pure magic. We got to skip school, watch games and practices, collect autographs, play catch in the evenings, and camp out in an RV. When I started skating, I brought my board along, practicing tricks in the parking lot while Big Mike and Big Al barbecued. My brother Bryce, Little Mike, and I spent those nights running around, carefree and invincible.

One evening, after a day game, I was skating in the now-empty parking lot. The fans, players, coaches, and staff had all gone home—at least, that's what we thought. Then we heard it: *crack*.

We froze. Bryce, Little Mike, and I looked at each other, unsure if we'd actually heard what we thought we did. A few moments of silence stretched into what felt like minutes. Then, *crack*—louder this time, echoing off the stadium walls. There was no mistaking it: the sound of a wooden bat meeting a baseball. Someone was still here.

Land on Both Feet

We grabbed our gloves, a ball, and a pen, hoping whoever it was might be a starter. But it was late, and the odds were slim—it was probably a single-, double-, or triple-A player getting in extra reps. Still, we followed the sound, cutting across the training grounds. *Crack!* "It's coming from the far back right field!" I yelled. We took off running, with our dads trailing behind.

When we got close, we saw him: a lone figure hitting baseballs off a tee. Not a pitcher throwing heat, not a coach lobbing BP—just a man, a bucket of balls, and a tee. For a moment, I thought I was imagining things. The stance, the swing, the follow-through—it couldn't be. Could it? Then it hit me all at once: *Tony f***ing Gwynn.*

The hitter of his generation, practicing the basics, like a Little Leaguer.

We did our best to play it cool as we approached, but Tony spotted us and waved us over. If you really know Tony, it's no surprise he welcomed us with a smile, chatting as he kept swinging. Big Mike, ever the teacher, asked why he was hitting off a tee. Without missing a beat, Tony replied, "I always go back to the basics after an off day." An off day? He'd gone 1-for-3 in the game earlier—hardly an off day by MLB standards.

We couldn't believe it. There we were, ten feet from one of the greatest hitters in baseball history, watching him hit balls off a tee. No cameras. No press. No teammates. Just us, Tony, and the crisp *crack* of the bat echoing into the night.

And then, the unthinkable: Tony ran out of balls. We assumed the session was over, but instead, he turned to us kids and said, "Don't just stand there—let's go! The night's not getting any younger." He opened the gate, and we ran onto the field, gathering up baseballs for Tony Gwynn.

After we loaded up the bucket, he went back to hitting. We stood there, mesmerized, watching him work through the night. That sound—*crack*—still rings in my ears sometimes.

Tony wasn't hitting for the crowd, his coaches, or even for us. He was doing it for himself. That night, on a quiet backfield in Peoria, he showed me the true meaning of dedication.

You'd think that experience would have cemented the value of practice in my brain forever. To be the best, you have to practice the basics—over and over again. But life is distracting, and our lofty goals can cloud our judgment. Sometimes it takes mistakes or missteps to learn life's lessons. Other times, wisdom is handed to us, but only if we're smart enough to listen.

The first step in building anything is laying the foundation: strength, balance, flexibility, control, vision, ambition. You establish that foundation through years of consistent practice, refining the basics until they're second nature.

Skaters are no different. If you can land a kickflip, heel flip, nosegrind, or tailslide nine out of ten times at home, you're on the right track. But you have to keep practicing them—even after you've moved on to harder tricks. Consistency is the key to progression.

This is the path to success: don't chase the hardest tricks or rush to film everything. Put in the work, refine your skills, and play your game. Companies hire people, not robots—your style and creativity are what make you unique.

Tony Gwynn wasn't a home run hitter. Stefan Janoski couldn't skate the biggest rails or do the hardest tricks. But they mastered their strengths and made their craft look effortless.

Land on Both Feet

It's not *what* you do—it's *how* you do it.

"Skateboarding isn't about fame or money. It's about love and the insane rush you get from nailing something you thought was impossible." ~ **Bam Margera**

9

Find Your Lane and Shred

In skateboarding, there are two ways to stand out: your bag of tricks and the way you do them. What makes skateboarding special is that there's no definitive GOAT. Sure, Tony Hawk has racked up contest wins and pushed vert skating further than anyone, but you can't compare him to a street skater. Skateboarding is a universe of styles: vert, pool, street, freestyle, park. Each requires a unique skill set, and the diversity within skating makes it nearly impossible to crown a single "greatest of all time."

Some skaters today bring a fresh perspective to the community, carving out their own lanes. Mark Suciu, Andy Anderson, and Franky Villani come to mind. Love them or hate them, they're undeniably different. They don't just stick to trendy tricks like bigspins and backside 180 nosegrinds—they do those too—but their trick selection and approach to skating set them apart. They make skateboarding feel less like a sport and more like an art form.

That said, if I had to call someone the GOAT, I'd say it without hesitation: Daewon Song.

Daewon isn't just a skateboarder; he's a visionary. Like Rodney Mullen before him, Daewon has consistently redefined what's possible in street skateboarding. His creativity knows no bounds. He looks at obstacles—traditional and nontraditional—and finds ways to skate them that no one else would ever consider. His technical skills are unmatched, but it's his imagination and artistry that truly set him apart.

Even at fifty years old, Daewon continues to drop mind-blowing skate clips on Instagram. His skating isn't just a showcase of talent; it's a masterclass in creativity and expression. Watching him skate reminds us that the limits of skateboarding are only as narrow as your imagination.

NBD

In skateboarding, NBD stands for "never been done." It's one thing that is always on our mind. There are three levels of NBDs.

The first is the true NBD: a trick no one, to common knowledge, has ever landed before. These are incredibly rare today. With decades of skateboarding history, finding something truly new is like striking gold. The second is a spot-specific NBD: a trick that's never been done at a particular ledge, stair set, or obstacle. It might not be groundbreaking globally, but it makes its mark on the spot's history. The third is the personal NBD: landing a trick you've never done before. It might not make headlines, but it's a milestone for you—and the feeling of achievement is just as real.

On my thirty-fifth skate day, I landed a personal NBD: a bigspin kickflip. It wasn't planned; it just kind of happened. I was skating a bump-to-gap near the end of the day, racing against the setting sun. I'd already gone through my usual rotation of flip tricks, but I still had eight or nine tricks to go to hit my goal of thirty-five.

The session was going well, but I was running out of ideas—and time. To keep the energy up, I threw a pressure flip up the gap as a joke (because, let's face it, no one takes that trick seriously). I even ollied up the gap while drinking a beer, which felt equal parts desperate and hilarious.

As the light faded, I decided to try something I'd never landed before. I'd already done a backside flip and a *tre flip* up the gap, so why not combine the two into a bigspin kickflip? It sounded doable—at least in theory.

The hard part about a bigspin kickflip is getting used to the rotation and the timing of the catch. My first few tries were total flings, nowhere close. But then something clicked. A few attempts later, I rolled away. It wasn't flawless, but it was solid—and for my first time ever doing the trick, I was pretty damn proud. Thirty-five years old and landing a new trick? Not bad for an "old dog."

True NBDs carry a special weight these days. Skateboarding's history is so rich that most tricks have already been created, refined, and filmed. In the early '90s, true NBDs were practically an everyday occurrence. Places like the World Industries warehouse, where Daewon skated, were hotbeds of innovation.

But even back then, NBDs weren't about staking a claim or making history. They were about exploration—pushing the boundaries of what you thought was possible.

Finding Your Lane

In the late '90s, Daewon Song embarked on an exploration that continues to this day. Driven by an insatiable need to innovate, he found a new lane—literally and figuratively. He began skating objects in ways no one had before.

One of Daewon's first revolutionary phases centered on picnic tables, a Southern California street-skating staple. Every skater knows which schools have the smaller tables —the ones just right for skating. Picnic tables are durable, smooth, and endlessly replaceable, making them immortalized spots as long as new tables are nearby.

While skaters had been using picnic tables for decades, Daewon took it to another level. He transformed them into elaborate setups: rows of eight as runways, angled tables as launch ramps, one on top for a manual pad, and another for the drop-down. The joke is that it probably took him longer to arrange the tables than to land the tricks. He didn't stop there—Daewon placed tables down stair sets, on roof gaps, and atop banks. If you can imagine a configuration, chances are he's already done it.

Daewon's drive to innovate was relentless. When standard ledges and rails no longer challenged him, he reinvented himself. There was his "nature phase," where he skated trees and rocks, using the woods as his playground. Later, he expanded his mini-ramp skating, adding bizarre obstacles to the sides of quarter pipes. Then came his "extreme" phase: switching wheels mid-air, landing tricks on multiple boards, or skating in the pouring rain with an umbrella.

That's Daewon: a creator. Arguably the most influential skater in history.

Watching Daewon's videos inspired me to find my lane, to see possibilities in the world around me. My friends and I spent hours at our Miramar setup spot, using whatever we could find: benches, barrels, fridge doors, wood pallets, sheet metal, truck beds. Those were some of my favorite skate memories—skating obstacles we built ourselves, ones no one else in the world would ever skate.

It's funny how experience changes your perspective. We can only see through the lens of our own understanding, and as that lens widens with time, so do the possibilities.

When I returned to the spots we skated as kids, I saw them with fresh eyes. Stairs and gaps we once obsessed over faded into the background as I noticed unique manual pads, curved ledges, and quirky architectural features we had overlooked.

I remember this one manual pad with an angle in the middle. It was barely wide enough to ride, and it twisted sharply before ending with a gap. Younger me wouldn't have touched it, but older me? I hit it for a manual kickflip —a trick I'd done countless times before but never in such a challenging spot.

We also found a ledge extending over grass and ending with a gap to curb. It was trickier to skate since the business park was open on weekends, but we found a solution: lugging a generator out one night to light the ledge. Skating at night added its own vibe—plus, the footage always looks cooler. That night, I landed a noseg-rind pop-over. In my mind, Marc Johnson would've approved.

As time passed, I began carving out my own lane in skateboarding. Big stair sets and rails became too hard on my body, so I leaned into creativity. I sought out unique manual pads with banks or curves, combining grinds, slides, and manuals into something uniquely mine. Bumps over cans, ledges across gaps, or weird architecture became my playground.

Following in Daewon's footsteps, I learned to embrace the style of skating I excelled at and enjoyed. If I hadn't spent so much time chasing the high-pressure path of the pros, I might have discovered my sweet spot much earlier.

Eventually, we all need to find our lane. And the only way to find it is to put in the work. Through trial and error, you'll figure out what drives you and what doesn't. That's where the magic happens—when you stop following someone else's path and start building your own.

NOW, SHRED

Discovering your lane might be the hardest part of life. I think back to freshman orientation, standing in that gym surrounded by hundreds of my future classmates. Where do I fit in? Not just socially, but in the bigger picture—where would I thrive? It's an overwhelming question to ask a young person still figuring out who they are. How are you supposed to know your place in the world when you don't even know everything it means to *be you* yet?

The answer? Go out and create. Explore. Try new things. The beauty of it is that one day, it all starts to make sense—as if you planned it. As if every choice was deliberate, every step intentional. The reality? You probably have no idea what you're doing half the time. And that's okay. That's part of the ride.

By the end of it, you'll look back and think, *Wow, if I'd known how this would play out, it might've felt impossible.* But you don't know. You discover it piece by piece, step by step, trick by trick.

Skateboarding is a perfect example of this—it's art, ability, and application all rolled into one. Like Picasso, whose Blue Period, Pink Period, Cubism, and Surrealism defined his legacy, skating allows for constant transformation and self-expression. Daewon Song is the Picasso of skateboarding. His evolution, creativity, and contributions have made him a legend. He's continually redefined what's possible, inspiring skaters worldwide.

But here's the truth: We can't all be Daewons or Picassos. That's not the point. Skateboarding thrives because it's a collective effort. Every day, kids push their limits, expanding what's possible. The older generation passes down their wisdom and experiences for others to build on. It's a cycle. When you realize we're all part of this global skate community, finding your place becomes more than just a personal mission—it becomes your way of giving back.

Find your lane. Follow your influences, but add your own flavor. Be yourself—your unique perspective is what sets you apart. A million people might have already done what you're trying to achieve, but no one's done it *your* way. That's what matters.

Commit to your approach. Practice, practice, practice. Through dedication and exploration, you'll find your sweet spot. When the time comes, seek out the undiscovered, embrace the unknown, and shred your lane.

"You didn't quit skateboarding because you got old; you got old because you quit skateboarding." ~ **Jay Adams**

10

Focus, Forget, and Always Land On Both Feet

You made it! Only two chapters left. Thanks for sticking it out this far. If you've skipped ahead to this chapter just because the book's title is in it—shame on you! But hey, I'm not here to stop you. Push forward, young squire.

So far, we've covered a lot: the lessons I've learned from my skateboarding journey, the discoveries made along the way, the community we share, and the difference between good skaters and great ones. Even if you're not a skater (yet), I hope you've gained a deeper understanding of skateboarding culture and maybe even thought about how to apply these lessons to your own life.

But there's one thing we haven't talked about yet: **execution**—what it actually takes to land a trick. Well, you've earned it. Let's dive in.

FOCUS

The first step to landing any trick is getting in *the zone*. You've heard it from coaches, teachers, parents—everyone.

But being "in the zone" isn't something you can force. It's a state where you're fully locked in, concentrating with everything you've got, and yet somehow, not consciously thinking at all.

How is that possible? How can you give something your full focus without actively thinking about it? The answer is practice. Lots of it.

To start, you need to understand your surroundings and your position within them. Then, think about your goal. Let's use a birthday skate session as an example. What's our short-term goal? Land the first trick of the day. And the larger, overarching goal? To land as many tricks as the number of years you've been alive by the end of the session.

Now, break it down further. What factors might jeopardize your ability to achieve the larger goal? Time and difficulty are usually the biggest hurdles. In this situation, time is critical. By analyzing both your immediate and long-term goals, you can approach the challenge rationally, with a clear plan. It's easy to feel motivated at the start, but once you're deep into the day's tricks, the mental and physical battle gets harder.

But for now, it's time to land that first trick.

Whether it's something you've done a million times or a personal NBD, it requires the same level of concentration. Nothing else should occupy your mind. Not overdue homework, not post-prom plans, not a job you're struggling with, not even a wedding you're hosting in twelve days. None of it matters right now.

You're present. You're prepared. You push up to the ledge and pop your first attempt. The battle has officially begun.

FORGET

Sometimes, letting go of the thoughts swirling around your head feels impossible—especially when life is hectic. For me, it's been a whirlwind. Fatherhood is no joke. We had our son, Aro, during the pandemic while temporarily living at my dad's house, on our way back to Austin. Not exactly how we pictured bringing a kid into the world, but what can I say? When one door closes, grind the steps.

But when I'm skating, I can't think about any of that. I can't let my mind wander to my wife stressing over sleepless nights or Aro's adorable smile. Good thoughts or bad, they've all got to sit on the sidelines. Getting distracted, even for a moment, is how you get hurt.

Luckily, for me, flipping that mental switch is second nature 99% of the time. The second I step on my board, the noise fades away. Years of skating have trained my brain to chase that feeling of freedom when life feels too heavy.

When I was younger, it wasn't so easy. I was constantly thinking ahead, worrying about my future. My goal at any given moment was to land the best trick I could, but my larger goal—turning pro—was always looming in the back of my mind. I knew big goals required small steps, but I didn't trust the process. Every failed trick felt like a step backward, like I was sliding further and further from the dream. I wasn't fully present in the moment because I was too distracted by the bigger picture.

These days, my skateboarding is different. My immediate goal is still to land tricks, but my larger goal is simply to enjoy the time I spend skating. The trick is balancing the two—because if I get too lost in chasing tricks, I risk sacrificing the joy of the session.

Take my thirty-seventh skate day, for example. I'd already landed twenty-six tricks at the first two parks we hit, and I was feeling great. With evening approaching, I knew we had time to hit two more parks. I decided to push myself a little harder at the next spot, going for some more difficult tricks.

That's when things started to unravel.

I was trying a nollie heelflip manual up a step-up gap to pad—a tricky move that requires just the right pop. After an hour of trying, I was frustrated and spiraling. I couldn't stop thinking about my thirty-fifth skate day, when I'd failed the same trick. My mind kept shouting, *If you don't land this now, you'll regret it just like last time.*

My attitude took over. I threw my board. Twice. No matter how much I tried to calm down, I couldn't let it go.

Finally, I sat down, defeated. It was getting dark, with maybe an hour left before the lights turned off. I had nine more tricks to land, and I couldn't stay stuck in that rut. I had to reset.

So I switched obstacles completely. I started simple: a tail slide. Within a few tries, I landed one. Then came a lip slide—boom. A nose grind—boom. A backside 5-0—boom. Just like that, I was back in the groove.

Feeling re-energized, I returned to the step-up gap. This time, I started with some warm-up tricks to build momentum: *nollie halfcab heelflip, halfcab heelflip, nollie tre flip.* Then I went back to the *nollie heelflip* manual.

And guess what? Ten minutes later, I nailed it.

How? How could I land it so quickly the second time around, when I was even more tired?

It's simple: I was present. I forgot about the frustration of my earlier attempts. I wasn't worrying about the bigger goal. My focus was locked on that moment, and that moment alone.

Skateboarding demands complete focus. You need to evaluate your previous attempts, sure, but then you have to let them go. Forget the past, forget the distractions, and forget the noise. Once your wheels hit the ground on the next try, it's just you, your board, and the trick in front of you.

THE MADNESS

You have to trust your gut. No matter how determined you are to land a trick, if something doesn't feel right—bail. It's part of the process.

Skateboarders often develop odd routines and quirks to stay focused. Some tap their boards twice, take off their hats and run their fingers through their hair, snap their fingers, or pop their boards up and down before trying a trick. We call this *the madness*.

Every skater's madness is different. Jamie Foy, for example, probably doesn't care if his board is backward. Nyjah Huston, on the other hand, steps onto his trucks in a very specific way to align his pressure points for perfect balance. Andrew Reynolds has a full-blown pre-trick ritual. It's not always the same, but it's based entirely on feeling. Sometimes it's tapping his board and dropping it just so. Other times it's rolling up to a handrail twenty times to scope out the approach—or obsessing over the swing of his arm.

At its core, the madness is about finding comfort and confidence. It's how skaters put themselves in the right mindset to commit to a trick. And while these rituals aren't exclusive to skateboarding, there's something about this sport that amplifies the madness.

For me, little things can throw me off. A crack near the takeoff, certain people watching, or certain people *not* watching. Sometimes I'll ride up to a rail far more times than necessary, just to get into a groove. Other times, I'll make a bet with a friend to add a little pressure. The madness is personal—it's whatever gets you to a place where you can fully focus.

But here's the thing: focus and rituals only take you so far. Eventually, you have to stick it.

"Sticking it" means committing to the trick. Whether it's scary to try or technically difficult, landing with both feet takes courage. You can half-commit all day, landing on one foot every time, but if you want to roll away, you have to go for it.

This is the moment we've been working toward.

We've learned the craft of skateboarding and the balance it requires. We know how to push, control, and gauge our speed. We've gotten up after hard slams and lived to ride another day. We've embraced falling and failing as essential parts of the process.

We understand that when the opportunity to land a trick presents itself, there's no guarantee of another try.

We've trained. We've practiced the basics until they're second nature. We've pushed our limits and quieted the distractions. We're focused entirely on the trick in front of us.

Now, it's time.

LFG!

LAND ON BOTH FEET

It's time.

Why else are we here? We didn't spend years training for this moment to give it fifty percent. We didn't choose skateboarding because it's safe. We didn't spend countless hours idolizing our favorite pros just to deny ourselves the chance to achieve what they've done.

We're here to go for it. To commit fully. To stick it.

Unless our gut tells us something is wrong, we don't bail—or at least we try not to. We're human, after all. Perfection isn't guaranteed. But one thing is certain: you can't roll away with one foot still on the ground. As the saying goes, "You can't steal second base with your foot still on first."

It's not just about having the courage to try. It's about being strong enough to handle failure when it comes—and it will come. That's why we've been training. As skateboarders, we're prepared for this, even if we don't realize it. Deep down, we carry a tenacity that's waiting to be put to use.

We've learned that failure isn't the end—it's part of the process. Every battle lost is knowledge gained. Falling doesn't mean the war is over; it means we've taken one more step forward. We've fallen hard, bounced back, and come out stronger every time.

Everything we've been through—the scraped knees, the hours of practice, the tricks that took days or weeks to land —has led to this moment. Whether it's our first time jumping a five-stair or filming the ender for a pro shoe video part, every experience we've had pays off now.

Committing to a trick can be the hardest part of skateboarding. But once you do, everything else falls into place. You don't even have to remind yourself to focus or forget— you're plugged into the zone, giving it one hundred percent.

And then, there's the best feeling in the world: knowing you're about to land a trick you've never done before. Not blind confidence, but something deeper—a wisdom honed through years of persistence and progression, paired with the confidence earned from practice. That certainty, that battle to make it happen, often feels even better than the roll away.

TOP OF THE HILL

In 2023, I turned forty. Spoiler alert: I didn't buy a million-dollar house. But I did build a skatepark in our backyard, and honestly, that felt even better. Yes, I still need a calendar to carve out time to skate, but it's worth it. My toddler, Aro, makes sure of that. It's pretty awesome—he'll point at the garage door where my skateboard is or grab my skate shoes from the laundry room and bring them to me. Who am I to argue with that kind of motivation?

On my 40th skate day, I was rounding out the last few tricks. This time, I decided to end with two specific tricks: a noseblunt slide and a fakie flip tailslide. Back in the day, these were some of my favorites, and I was pretty good at them. Now, I wanted to land them as someone officially "over the hill."

I have a bump-to-setup box in the backyard that seemed perfect for the noseblunt. The first few tries weren't even close—I wasn't committing to putting all my weight on the nose of the board. It was intimidating, even after all these years. But then, on one attempt, I locked in and slid halfway down the box.

It was *go time.*

A rush of energy surged through me. This wasn't a trick I'd never done before, but I hadn't tried it in at least five years—and never on this setup. A few attempts later, I slid across the whole box. I knew it was just a matter of time before I landed it.

Something about that moment felt different. I was

focused, sure—but I also felt a deep appreciation for the process. I paused to think, *I'm forty years old, and I'm about to noseblunt the hell out of this ledge. How awesome is that?*

A few tries later, I landed it. And it felt *incredible*.

I was so pumped that I wanted to do it again—and again. I must have landed six or seven more before moving on to my last trick. I probably shouldn't have burned so much energy, but I didn't care. I wanted to soak in the moment, reliving it with every successful attempt.

Riding that high, I started on the fakie flip tailslide on a flat box. To my surprise, it took me fewer than ten tries. The first time I locked in, muscle memory kicked in, and it just clicked.

With that, I finished my forty tricks and threw my hands in the air, victorious.

That day, everything just made sense. It was one of those rare moments in life where everything feels perfectly aligned. I'll forever look back on it with gratitude and pride.

The Beginning of the End

Similar to my 40th skate day, this day—nearly 20 years earlier—was arguably the best skateboarding day of my life. But the real surprise came with the realization I had afterward.

At the peak of my skateboarding journey, I found myself at a school in downtown San Diego. It was one of those perfect Southern California days—sunny, breezy, with temperatures in the 70s. Everything about it felt right. My goal that day was ambitious: a frontside boardslide on a handrail that was taller, and longer than anything I'd tackled before. At this stage of my journey, the dream of becoming a professional skateboarder was still crystal clear.

A few friends and I arrived at the school, only to find Mark Appleyard already skating the set. Legendary for his effortless style, Mark makes even the hardest tricks look like a casual stroll. It was intimidating, but when he greeted us with a friendly "hello," the tension eased. I started warming up as my buddy Ryan set up the camera. If I was going to film a trick with Mark Appleyard there, I had to commit to it *first T*. Despite the rail's intimidating size, I landed the front boardslide fairly easily—the biggest rail I'd ever skated. I was buzzing.

Then, things got even more surreal. My friend Charlie Castelluzzo hopped the fence to join us. Charlie, a little powerhouse of a skater, was already sponsored and filming for a video part. With him was a filmer from Pacific Drive, the iconic San Diego skate shop. Not long after, Brandon Turner rolled up—a pro I knew from my time working at Osiris, a shoe company that sponsored him. Suddenly a casual skate day turned into a full blown session. The energy was electric.

Everyone had their eyes on their own challenges. Charlie attempted a switch crook on the rail, but it slipped away from him. Brandon tried a nollie backside flip down the stairs—a trick so insane it barely felt real. The energy from the session was contagious. I landed a front board fakie and, later, a smith grind—tricks I hadn't even planned to try. I had never done a front board fakie before on a hand rail, and getting up to lock in on a smith grind I never thought I could do. Everything felt effortless, like I was operating on instinct alone.

There's nothing like the energy of a great skate session. Everyone pushes each other, cheering for every near-miss

Land on Both Feet

and celebration-worthy make. After I landed the smith grind, Charlie urged me to try a nosegrind. He knew my strengths, and he knew this rail would be monumental for me. It was a monster in height, and a nosegrind on it was the definition of a "hammer."

I rolled up a few times, sizing it up. From the base of the rail, it loomed tall, almost impossible. But I knew the only way to beat it was to commit. At the top of the runway, I glanced at my friends—Mark, Brandon, Charlie—and muttered, "Fuck it." I threw my board down and pushed hard.

I popped as high as I could, aiming for the rail. My front truck locked in, and I floated over the stairs. *I bailed*, hitting the cement, and tucked into a roll to ease the impact. At that moment, I knew it was possible—I knew I was going to land it.

Maybe six tries later, I locked in with my weight on top. It felt right. Not perfect, but right. I landed with a little tic-tac but knew I could do better. Ryan Muller, my filmer that day, played back the clip—and that's when we realized the camera battery had died mid-trick. No footage. My heart sank. What's the point of landing the best trick of your life if no one can see it?

Thankfully, Charlie's filmer offered to stay and shoot it for me, even after Charlie had slammed and called it a day. I couldn't waste his time or this opportunity. I was so grateful and told him that I was going to land it next try..

With the camera rolling, I approached the rail again. The moment I popped, time seemed to slow. My front truck locked in, and everything felt balanced—effortless, even. I could feel the rail beneath me, the grind of metal carrying me all the way to the end. As I reached the final inches, I gave the board a slight nudge off the rail—just a little extra sauce. My feet stayed glued to the deck as I stomped the landing on all four wheels and rolled away.

It was surreal—simultaneously happening in a split second and stretching into an eternity. That trick wasn't just the best of my life; it was the culmination of everything I'd worked for, every session, every slam, every "one more try." For that moment, I was invincible.

It was the happiest moment of my life—up to that point. I stayed on my board until the momentum stopped me completely, refusing to let the moment end. The roll-away is one of the greatest feelings in skateboarding. It's hard to explain, this nebulous mix of jubilation and release. Sometimes you laugh, sometimes you cheer, sometimes you cry. That day, I just stayed on my board, savoring every second the momentum allowed.

Everyone there gave me props. The filmer transferred me the clip, and I sat down to watch it over and over, as if I needed to prove to myself that it wasn't just a dream. It was real. This was my reality. My dream felt within reach, closer than ever.

It was a quintessential San Diego day—not a cloud in the sky, the kind of day that makes you feel invincible. But as we packed up, hopped the school fence, and walked to the car, a thought struck me that would change everything: *This might be the best trick I'll ever do.*

I don't know where the thought came from, but it felt profound. It didn't diminish the accomplishment. If anything, it allowed me to appreciate it even more. But it also posed a question I wasn't ready for: *What does that mean for me?*

I knew I wasn't as good as some of the average professionals out there. Skating alongside guys like Mark Appleyard, Brandon Turner, and my friend Charlie Castelluzzo

Land on Both Feet

made that clear. They were more talented, more consistent. And for months, I'd been standing at a crossroads. If I wanted to chase the dream of going pro, I'd need to drop out of college and dedicate my entire life to skateboarding. It meant giving up everything else for a shot at a career I wasn't sure I could sustain.

The other path was safer, but not easier. I could stay in school, keep skating for the love of it, and build a career outside the skate world. I'd still push myself, still progress, but I'd know deep down that skating would never be more than a passion. That path meant letting go of a lifelong dream—to be a professional athlete.

I had already given up baseball and soccer to skateboard, pouring myself into it for seven years. I'd landed sponsorships, broken into the right circles, and proven I had potential. Logically, landing one of my idol Marc Johnson's signature tricks should have cemented my motivation to go all in. But as I watched the clip one last time, sitting on the curb under that perfect San Diego sky, the answer was clear: *I'm done chasing this dream.*

And to my surprise, I was okay with that. More than okay—I felt at peace.

From that day forward, I stayed in school. I kept my sponsors, competed in events, and continued skating progressively through college. Eventually, the sponsors fizzled out as life took shape. I never stopped skating, though, and I don't intend to until my legs or body give out. But that day, I let go of the dream of turning pro—and it was one of the best days of my life.

It sounds strange, I know. Realizing your childhood

dream isn't going to happen and calling it the best day of your life? But that's exactly what it was. That trick on the rail wasn't just about skateboarding. It was the culmination of years of work, of every late-night session learning to ollie, every backyard experiment with friends, every hour watching skate videos and emulating my heroes. It was the apex of my skateboarding life, and landing that trick felt like a victory over everything I'd doubted about myself.

Without experience, failure is terrifying. Most people either avoid trying or hold back, so they can't fully blame themselves when they fall short. It's self-protection. Skateboarders don't have that luxury. We fail constantly—hundreds, thousands of times—but we learn to embrace it. We seek it out, on the board and off. That mindset leads so many skaters to become entrepreneurs, creatives, and innovators. We're willing to take risks and face the consequences. We know failure is part of growth.

Skateboarding teaches precision, discipline, and resilience. It sharpens you into someone who can teach, inspire, and pass those lessons to the next generation. It's more than just a sport; it's a way of seeing the world—and yourself.

Life is short. It feels like only months ago I was a teenager skating flat bars with my friends. You blink, and half your life is gone. My grandfather didn't live past his sixties. My mom was one of the healthiest people I knew, and she passed in her early sixties from stage-four cancer. I still dream about her—dreams where she's alive, where I can share my life with her. Waking up from those dreams feels like getting punched in the gut, over and over again.

Skateboarding is what I turn to when I need to escape, to think, to feel alive. It taught me to see opportunity, even when it's not obvious. I wish my mom had been at my wedding. I wish she'd met her grandkids. I wish she could read this book. But life doesn't stop for wishes. When you're knocked down, you have to get back up, keep your head high, and look for the next chance.

Focus. Forget. And always land on both feet.

$\sim$

*"The moment you land a trick you've been chasing for hours, all the pain and frustration vanish. It's pure magic." ~ **Tony Hawk***

11

The Last Try Is a New Beginning

"Last try." I threw that phrase around a little too casually. I can't pinpoint where I picked it up or when I started saying it, but it stuck. After an hour of filming, when hope of landing a trick felt like it was slipping away, the words *last try* would echo from my tired diaphragm. My friends—usually crouched in some awkward bush, filming me for far longer than they'd signed up for—knew better. They understood the odds of it truly being my last attempt were slim to none.

The intention was always there, though. One last try. A final push. But the reality? It rarely worked out that way. If I was close to landing the trick, why stop? The "last try" was reserved for those moments when the trick seemed to have the upper hand over my mind.

Trying a trick for that long takes its toll. It's nearly impossible to stay focused. Exhaustion sets in—your legs are shot, your mind is drained. Think about how you feel after a tough workout or spin class. By the end, you're pleading with the clock to move faster, just going through the motions and praying for it to end. Skateboarding feels the same way. After enough tries, you're not controlling the board anymore—the board is controlling you.

Back to my 35th birthday: my nollie inward heelflip manual battle was the perfect example. After what felt like hours, my legs were toast, and my patience had long since vanished. My thoughts were a chaotic mix of frustration: *I still have thirty tricks to land today. Bryan's losing patience. These razor kids won't get out of my way. I'm pissed off, and I already know I'm not going to land it unless I get lucky.*

But giving up? That's just not in my nature. So I told Bryan, "Five more tries, I swear."

Four tries came and went. I wasn't any closer. I didn't even flip the board right, let alone land in a manual. "Last try," I muttered reluctantly, rolling past Bryan one more time. Turning around, I closed my eyes and took a deep breath. *This is the one. If I just dig deep, focus, and give it everything, I can land it.*

I threw my board down, pushed toward the launch ramp, and positioned my feet perfectly. As I hit the incline, I crouched low and popped at just the right moment, flicking with my back heel. I could tell instantly that this flick was clean. The board flipped smoothly beneath me as I floated over the gap. I caught it perfectly, landing in manual with my nose slightly elevated. For a second, it felt locked in—until my balance gave out, and my front wheels hit the ground. *Shit. So close.*

Without thinking, I blurted, "I had it. One more—last try, I swear." And just like that, the can of worms cracked open. If that wasn't the last try, this next one probably wouldn't be either.

That day, I only gave it a few more attempts before conceding. But I paid the price shortly after. Trying to lipslide a rail off a drop that extended over a ledge, I had to swerve around Bryan, who was filming while skating alongside me. Exhaustion from the earlier battle caught up with me, and I didn't pop right. I got sacked on the rail—a harsh reminder of the physical and mental toll of pushing too far.

The Meaning of "Last Try"

For me, "last try" is an attempt to grab control of a spiraling situation. It's doubling down when the clock is running out and forcing myself to give one final, worthy attempt. Whether it's my mind or my emotions unraveling, saying "last try" is my way of hitting reset. It's a chance to clear out the frustration, doubt, and anger of the past twenty minutes and focus everything I have on just one attempt.

Sometimes it works. Sometimes I manage to recenter myself, regain control, and land the trick. Other times, slipping back into the gutter is inevitable. But that's the beauty of the "last try"—it's not just about the trick. It's about the process. It's about finding the strength to push forward when everything feels stacked against you. Skateboarding, like life, is full of setbacks and failures. The "last try" isn't always about landing the trick; sometimes it's about proving to yourself that you gave it everything. And when it works—when you land that elusive trick on your last try— it's not just a victory. It's a new beginning.

The One That Got Away

There's a well-known four-block just outside Chino Hills at a baseball field—the perfect stair set to film a trick. Legendary, even. Every pro had skated this spot, landing incredible tricks down the set. I'd never done a half-cab heelflip down anything bigger than a four-stair, and this one was closer to an eight. Still, that little voice on my shoulder whispered: *You've got this.* And to make it even better, I had never seen a pro land that specific trick on the set. As far as I knew, it could have been an NBD.

I wanted to do a line—landing more than one trick back-to-back. Lines are harder; they require you to hit every trick in succession without messing up. At the top of the set was a two-stair. Not many people attempted lines at Chino Hills, and I thought it'd be cool to change that. My plan: start with a nollie backside heelflip on the two-stair, then hit the half-cab heel on the big four.

I didn't land it. Not that day or the next two times I returned. Across three trips, I must have landed on the trick at least fifteen times but never rode away clean. I remember that last day vividly. I slammed hard a few times, frustration building with every failed attempt. The idea of coming back to try again felt unbearable. I told myself, *This is it. This is the last time I'll ever skate this spot. If I'm going to land this trick, it has to be now.*

I'll save you the suspense: I didn't land it. And yes, I kept trying, claiming each attempt was my last. By the end of the day, my thoughts were so scrambled I couldn't focus. It's hard to block out the voice in your head telling you you're not good enough after so many failed tries. Ironically, I don't even remember how I finally called it quits— seems I was better at blocking *that* part out.

Another battle I lost happened at the Santa Monica Courthouse, back before it was converted into a skatepark. It was a mecca of obstacles: a long five-stair, a normal four-stair, ledges, and a giant manual pad that barely anyone could ollie onto. My friend Casey Rigney—one of the most talented skaters I knew—pulled off a nollie heelflip nose manual on it. This was before Instagram, so barely anyone saw it, but it was absolutely bananas.

I had orchestrated a line to film that day. I can't remember the whole thing because I never made it past the first trick: a fakie flip crook. I'd only landed one or two in my life, so naturally, I wanted to film one. In hindsight, I should've practiced it more. But my impatience got the better of me, and I went straight into filming. The plan was risky: put the hardest trick first, so I wouldn't frustrate the filmer if I bailed later in the line.

Big mistake.

I kept trying for over thirty minutes, but my flips were inconsistent, and I wasn't even getting onto the ledge properly. By the end of the session, I was mentally and physically drained. Frustration bubbled over. I thought, *Screw it. Last try. I'm going for it.*

Famous last words.

On that final attempt, I slipped out, fell hard, and cracked four metacarpals in my left hand. Game over. I popped my hand back into place, wrapped it in a T-shirt, and tried to play it cool. No dramatic yelps, no embarrassing noises—just the quiet defeat of knowing my day was done.

That slam sidelined me for a month, but I came back. That's what skateboarding is: trying, failing, and coming back stronger. It's a cycle that teaches you more about yourself than any single success ever could. Growth comes through adversity. It's in the moments when you're tired, beaten, and defeated that your drive is truly tested.

When you think you can't push any further, that's when you find out who you are. Your limits aren't fixed—they stretch like elastic. The more you push, the more resistance you feel. But if you dig deep, you can go further than you ever thought possible.

The last try isn't just about skateboarding. It's the final rep of a workout, the last few steps of a hundred-meter dash, the red zone offense in the fourth quarter. It's a full count with the bases loaded. The last try is where history is made. It's also where you loosen your grip on control and fight to reclaim it.

The last try is always a new beginning. Whether you slam or roll away, you're faced with a choice: *What now?* If you failed, are you willing to quit, or will you come back better prepared? If you succeed, is that enough, or will you keep pushing for perfection?

For me, this question—*what comes after the last try?*—is the closest I've come to understanding my purpose. Personal fulfillment lies in the balance between the pursuit of future growth and the appreciation of the present. The last try is always a new beginning. What you do next is entirely up to you.

~

"The best feeling in the world is landing something you've been working on for days, weeks, or even months. That's what makes it all worth it." ~ Chris Cole

The Final Push

Skateboarding has taught me a lot—about balance, resilience, creativity, and the importance of slamming face-first into the pavement every now and then. But perhaps the biggest lesson is this: life rolls by fast and picks up speed every day. Don't let it pass you by.

As skaters, we obsess over the smallest details. *My arm looked weird after landing. I lost too much speed on the rollaway. That crook wasn't pinched enough. I didn't catch the flick right.* We chase perfection, even though deep down, we know it doesn't exist.

But here's the thing—even the pros, the ones who make everything look effortless, are just as self-conscious. They might land a trick ten times before finally getting the one they use in their video part.

I used to think the *sponsor-me* video was everything. I wanted a part that could hold its own among the best, so maybe—just maybe—I could be like them one day. But I've learned that the real magic isn't in the final clip. It's in the battles. The slams that leave your knees raw. The sunset sessions with the homies. The early morning missions before the city wakes up. It's in the awkward, mongo-pushing kid who reminds you where you started.

Life is no different. We're all out here trying to land something—whether it's a promotion, a relationship, or just making it to Friday without losing it. And just like skating, life is unpredictable. You never know when you're going to get wheelbite. Sometimes you land perfectly on the bolts. Sometimes you slam so hard you wonder if you'll ever get back up. But every attempt adds to a story that's uniquely yours.

The truth is, there's no perfect endgame. Just when you think Jamie Foy's front crook down El Toro 20 couldn't be topped, he finds some long triple-kink rail to one-up himself. There's always a bigger gap, a bigger rail, another set of stairs to take on. It's up to you to keep pushing your limits.

Find the joy in every push, every pop, every spot you roll up to. Skateboarding—and life—are about momentum. It's about how you move through the world, how you adapt when things get rough, and how you keep going when your legs are shot and your board feels like it's fighting you.

And if you ever find yourself staring at a rail you're too scared to hit, or a goal that feels impossible, remember this: you've already rolled up to the spot. You've already envisioned what you want to do. That's the hardest part.

Now all that's left is to commit.

Push with your back foot. The rest will come naturally.

SEE YOU OUT THERE.

Brett Soren